Basics of Writing for the Mass Media

Marlan D. Nelson
Oklahoma State University

George R. Rhoades
University of Texas at Arlington

Foreword by Harry Heath Jr.

KENDALL/HUNT PUBLISHING COMPANY
Dubuque, Iowa

Cover design by Warren Niece

This edition has been printed directly from the authors' manuscript copy

Copyright © 1984 by Kendall/Hunt Publishing Company

Library of Congress Catalog Card Number: 83-82712

ISBN 0-8403-3213-0

All rights reserved. No part of this publication may be reproduced, stored in a retrieval system, or transmitted, in any form or by any means, electronic, mechanical, photocopying, recording, or otherwise, without the prior written permission of the copyright owner.

Printed in the United States of America

B   403213   01

Contents

Foreword, by Dr. Harry Heath, Jr., vii
From the Authors, ix

Chapter
1. **Communication: What Is It?**, 1
   What Is Communication, 1
   The Communication Process, 2
   How Communication Has Effects, 3
   Communication Hurdles, 4
   Exercises, 7
2. **What Is News?**, 9
   Timeliness, 9
   Proximity, 10
   Prominence, 10
   Impact, 10
   Human Interest, 11
   Combination of Characteristics, 12
   Exercises, 13
3. **News Story Structure**, 15
   Inverted Pyramid, 15
   Chronological Order, 18
   Suspended Interest, 19
   Summary Leads, 19
   Unity, 23
   Multi-Dimensional, 24
   Exercises, 27
4. **Refining the News Story**, 31
   Sentence Structure, 31

    Modifiers, 32
    Parallel Construction, 33
    Common Mistakes, 33
    Specificity and Conciseness, 40
    Handling Quotes, 41
    Direct Quotes, 42
    Indirect Quotes, 44
    Verbs of Attribution, 44
    Where to Place Attribution, 45
    Speeches, 47
    Pre-Speech Story, 48
    Speech Story Example, 49
    Exercises, 51

5. **Broadcast Style, 55**
    Exercises, 58

6. **Interviewing for the Media, 65**
    Direct Observation, 65
    Secondary Sources, 66
    Interviewing, 66
    Pre-Interview Research, 68
    The Interview, 69
    Non-Directed Questions, 70
    Directed Questions, 71
    Success in Interviewing, 74
    Telephone Interviews, 76
    Taking Notes, 77
    Exercises, 78

7. **References for Journalists, 79**
    News Digests, 79
    Fact Finders, 80
    Directories, 80
    Newspaper Indexes, 82
    Periodical Indexes, 82
    Biographical Sources, 83
    Dictionaries and Word Books, 84

Quotation Books, 85
Local Directories, 85
Yearbooks, 86
Computer-Based Data Systems, 87
Books in Print, 87
Exercises, 88

8. **Feature Writing, 89**
Features Defined, 89
Entertaining Features, 91
Feature Story Development, 91
Types of Features, 91
The Lead, 94
The Body of the Feature, 98
Feature Endings, 100
Exercises, 105

9. **Advertising: the Support System, 107**
The Advertising Process, 109
Copy Approaches: Factual, 110
Emotional Copy, 112
Exercises, 115

10. **Public Relations, 117**
Communication Theory and PR, 117
Writing the PR Release, 118
Exercises, 120

11. **Editing Media Copy, 123**
Editing Words, 124
Editing Sentences, 125
Active Voice, 126
Faulty Construction, 127
Editing Stories, 128

12. **Basic Legal Concepts, 131**
Libel, 131
Three Major Defense, 132
Other Defenses, 133
Malice, 133

Invasion of Privacy, 133
Exercises, 134
Appendix A, SPJ Code, 135
Appendix B, Copyreading Symbols, 139
Appendix C, Copyreading for Broadcasting, 143
Appendix D, Spelling Demons, 145
Appendix E, News Story Format, 150
Appendix F, PR Release, 153
Index, 155

Foreword...

This is an imminently practical book. It comes at a time when the differences among media in their writing styles are becoming less pronounced. This trend, slowly evolving for at least four decades, will continue. It will be accelerated by electronically based computer-driven information systems. These systems are having a profound effect upon the delivery of information to both mass and specialized audiences, and more and more emphasis will be placed upon clear, concise writing to feed these marvelous new tools. The connection between the new technology and the goals of this book should be self-evident.

The nature of the book has been influenced, too, by the obvious slippage in communications skills among students from many, if not most, public schools. Thus the use of exercises to reinforce forgotten or never-learned punctuation, grammar and spelling.

On a more personal note, one of my goals in becoming director of the Oklahoma State University School of Journalism and Broadcasting in 1967—a position now held by one of this book's co-authors—was to establish what I called a cross-media approach to journalistic writing. I started what was perhaps the first course in a major journalism school to take this approach. The reason: the differences in writing for the media had been over-emphasized for too long; the similarities had been under-emphasized or overlooked. In the expensive atmosphere of media studies today, we can ill afford a beginning writing course for each of the media. Properly taught, a course using this textbook can offer a foundation for the more advanced writing courses the student will encounter, whether for print or the telecommunicative media.

The authors have had excellent preparation professionally and academically for the work they have undertaken with **Basics of Writing for the Mass Media.** They are on the right track, in my opinion, and so will their readers be, if they love the language and the power it has to evoke images, clarify issues, and report accurately upon the events of our time. I cannot state too strongly the importance of accurate, balanced, substantive reportage as we approach a new century with its global challenges. This course, for many, will be the first step toward that high calling.

> HARRY HEATH
> Regents Service Professor
> Oklahoma State University

From the Authors...

We have prepared this book to serve as a text for an introductory course in mass media writing. We believe that a unified approach which stresses traditional journalism news style as well as broadcasting, public relations, advertising and other areas is needed for today's prospective journalist. Technology and other advances have led to the merging of media writing techniques, and we hope this book will contribute to training professionals to meet the new demands.

A word about the language used in the textbook may be beneficial. The authors recognize the concern for the sexist use of the male pronouns and beg the reader's understanding in going along with such usage. Casting language to include both genders of pronouns is awkward and results in somewhat stilted presentation. The male gender pronouns are used in this text, not as male, but as neutral expressions.

The authors express their appreciation to contributions made by several people. First, we acknowledge the support and inspiration of Dr. Harry Heath Jr., former director of the School of Journalism and Broadcasting at Oklahoma State University. Dr. Heath was one of the first journalism educators to develop an integrated writing for media course, and he gave the authors encouragement to undertake the project.

Others in the professional and academic worlds who contributed to the education and training of the authors were Dr. Walter Ward, Oklahoma State University; James C. Stratton and Lemuel D. Groom, professor emeriti, Oklahoma State University; Alex Adwan, associate editor of the Tulsa World; Travis Hughs, vice president, UPI; Paul McClung, managing editor of the Lawton (Okla.) Constitution; Ed Carter, associate professor of journalism, Univerity of Oklahoma; Dr. Carlton F. Culmsee, dean emeritus, College of Humanities and Arts, Utah State University; the late C.A. "Cab" Burley of the Menlo Park (Calif.) Recorder; the late R. S. Pennington, publisher of the Haskell (Okla.) News; Dr. M. Judd Harmon, dean emeritus, College of Humanities, Arts and Social Sciences, Utah State University, and the hundreds of reporting students who have contributed to our education.

Thanks are also expressed to Leland Tenney, business manager of the Daily O'Collegian, Oklahoma State University, for help in type design; Carla Greiner for help in layout; Jone Hawkins and Tanya Turner for manuscript typing and Warren Niece for the cover design.

And finally we want to thank our wives—Lynn Rhoades and Mary Louise Nelson—and the Nelson children, Steve and Linda, for their special understanding and support during the preparation of this book.

Stillwater, Oklahoma
September 15, 1983
Marlan D. Nelson
George R. Rhoades

Communication: What Is It?

Writing for the mass media involves three distinct steps: research, thinking and writing. A person who sits down at the typewriter before taking the first two steps is like a surgeon who begins a complex operation before learning human physiology, chemistry and how to use the basic instruments. The "writer" like the "surgeon," might accomplish the task, but the procedure may kill the patient.

Media writers research a topic as well as the audience to whom the information (message) is directed to achieve the ultimate goal of communication: tangible results. These results, frequently the same as the basic roles of the media, are to inform, to influence, to entertain and to sell goods and services.

Americans are dependent upon the mass media to provide information for making decisions about social, political and economic issues. This dependency places a significant burden upon the practitioners: they must search out issues facing mass man and through some near-magic "goad" him into reading or listening to the messages. To keep mass man informed, media writers are called upon, not only to write news reports linguistically correct, but to develop "packaging" for the product to attract readers and listeners. To accomplish this, writers turn to communication theory and to basic psychology. Central to transmitting messages is communicating to produce understanding. Let's turn now to consider what we mean by "understanding" and to the concepts of communication, the psychological factors in communication packaging and their ramifications.

What is Communication?

Many definitions for communication exist. Basically, communication—the essence of the mass media profession—involves what may be termed two worlds: the empirical world and the symbolic world, or put another way, the worlds of language and of reality. The empirical world represents things we experience through the senses of seeing, hearing, smelling, touching and tasting—the world represented by tangible objects, people, events, situations. The symbolic world is the world which we present through assigning symbols (words, pictures, gestures, philosophical stereotypes) to represent ideas, attitudes, basic values. The symbolic world is the one from which language developed.

Communication is so much a part of our everyday vocabulary that rarely do we stop to give attention to its meaning. However, the mass media writer who understands the term is better able to put together news and feature stories, television documentaries and special reports and advertising messages that break the confusion barrier and provide understanding for the reader/viewer/listener.

We can turn to a dictionary to find the denotative meaning of communication: **Webster's Ninth New Collegiate Dictionary** gives the denotative meaning: **an act or instance of transmitting** or **a process by which information is exchanged between individuals through a common system of symbols, signs or behaviors. (Used by permission. From Webster's Ninth New Collegiate Dictionary c 1983 by Merriam-Webster Inc., publishers of the Merriam-Webster Dictionaries.)**

Communication, too, can be defined from the Latin **Communis** which means common. Thus, if we add the derivation definition to the second part of the definition listed above, we come up with a meaning that describes the fundamental goal of media writing: a process by which information is exchanged between individuals through symbols, signs, or behavior, and which is designed to build a common background about a particular event for the writer, the source and the reader/viewer/listener. The significant two words in the broader definition are "a process."

For ideas, values, information and philosophies to be transmitted via the mass media, three basic elements are necessary: the source, the message and the destination. The source is the individual or the medium, the message is the information transmitted, and the destination is the reader/viewer/listener.

In the process of communication, the reporter aims a message at an audience; the purpose is to produce tangible results or effects. The reporter for radio, television, newspaper or magazine must present the message so that each receiver views it as directed to him and derives a similar meaning. That's quite an expectation. So how does the reporter go about accomplishing the basic goal?

The Communication Process

Communication researchers tell us that effective communication is a process by which senders and receivers are brought together philosophically.

The process involves building a bridge of understanding, so to speak, between sender and receiver. If we turn to the symbolic and empirical worlds of communication, we can explain how communication with understanding takes place. The empirical world of the news source, the news writer and the reader/viewer/listener represent tangible items that are seen, heard, smelled, felt or tasted. In a one-on-one or face-to-face situation, the sender and the receiver have little difficulty in understanding, for example, that a car ran over a child as they watched from a house across the street. The difficulty—and the real test—comes as we move to the symbolic world.

The reporter talks with a policeman who investigated the accident. The reporter takes the information and writes a news story for this afternoon's newspaper. The story communicated through words on white newsprint is read by several hundred-thousand people. The simplicity of communication—telling the story to someone—is still there; however, the meaning attached to the message--the understanding of the event--will depend upon how much "commonness" exists among the principals involved in this simple act of communicating.

To ensure a greater degree of universality to the message, the writer will attempt to research the event from as many angles as possible. The reporter's research is designed to help build a "frame of reference" or sufficient background so the reader/viewer/listener "sees" the event as near as possible to the way the reporter saw it. To build the frame of reference necessary to understand messages, reporters must be as knowledgeable as possible about topics and have an indepth understanding of the audience. Reporters who meet these two requisites will be able to communicate understanding to their audiences because the frames of reference of the two key groups have been refined.

How Communication Has Effects

Communication, as we have learned, is a process, and its ultimate goal is to produce effects or results. News stories are written to give readers/viewers/listeners vital information; editorials are written to give reader/viewers/listeners information to help to arrive at consensus; advertisements are broadcast and published to help create product desire or to urge one to buy. For messages to be effective, writers must understand the basic psychological factors related to effective communication. Let us now turn to a short review of some of those facts.

Communication Hurdles

Communication researchers tell us that there are four basic conditions which must be met if mass media messages are to be successful. Dr. Wilbur Schramm, in his book **The Process and Effects of Mass Communication**, lists four conditions or hurdles which messages must clear if they are to be effective: (1) the message must attract attention; (2) the message must be interpreted; (3) the message must arouse personality needs and suggest ways to meet the needs, and (4) the message must be stored.*

Let us look briefly at each of the "hurdles" and how they relate to writing for the mass media.

The Message Must Attract Attention

The writer's concern is to induce readers/listeners/viewers to see or hear the message. First, it must be made available; second, it must contain cues that relate to interests of potential receivers, and third it must be presented when readers/listeners/viewers have time to pay attention.

Overcoming these hurdles is part of the packaging of mass media messages. Packaging is essential because mass man is bombarded with messages via radio, television, newspapers, magazines, direct mail, telephone calls, books, movies, etc. And in our complex society, man is occupied with such day-to-day problems as making a living, raising a family and any number of so-called existence issues. Mass man is pre-occupied, and he can turn to numerous sources for information. Or he can remain uninformed. To draw him away from his pre-occupation, the media writer uses large, bold headlines, special attention-demanding sounds, intriguing lead writing styles, warm and cool colors, human interest pictures and special visual designs. These packaging devices are designed to draw the reader/listener/viewer into a story, and they are effective only to the extent that they identify with the receiver's interests.

The Message Must Be Interpreted

Once interest has been created, the writer develops the story to sustain interest. Put another way, the media writer must present the story to refer to

*Wilbur Schramm, The Process and Effects of Mass Communications. Urbana, Ill.: University of Illinois Press, 1955, pp. 3-10, 13-17.

experience or ideas shared by the reporter and the reader/listener/viewer. Too, the story must be written in language that is readily understandable. One must design messages using the same language as the receiver. In short, journalists must become so attuned to their audience that they strike a happy medium in language usage. The well educated and the person with a limited education must feel comfortable with the language. Psychologists tell us that messages must not conflict with the audience's philosophical views as well.

The Message Must Arouse Personality Needs and Suggest Some Way to Meet Them

Sustaining the interest of the reader/listener/viewer is achieved by appealing to basic personality needs of all humans. Thus, if one wants readers/listeners/viewers to zero-in on an advertisement, a news or feature story, or a television documentary, he relates the message to these psychological needs. One must show how those needs can be met by buying an advertised product or using the information in a story. The basic needs are security, status, belongingness, understanding, freedom from constraint, love and freedom from anxiety. They are self-explanatory and can be used to individualize mass audience messages.

The Message Must Suggest a Way to Meet Personality Needs Acceptable to the Receiver's Group Norms

Normative standards of groups in which one lives are other factors to be considered in predicting message effectiveness. From early life one lives in groups and learns standards and values from family, church, social, community, regional and national associations and identifications. Attitudes, values and opinions are influenced more strongly by group leaders than by media messages. Therefore, if news stories, advertisements, editorials and other media messages are to be effective, the writers must understand the group standards and present messages that are consistent with the way readers/listeners/viewers see the world. In other words, the effective writer must know the audience. To accomplish this, reporters rely on such things as community survey research and demographics. Thus, the reporter's message involves carefully researched details packaged for a target audience.

The hurdles described above are, broadly speaking, basic elements of mass communication theory. A knowledge of basic theory is needed by all who expect to enter the media professions. Theory is not a panacea. . . it makes the writer conscious of how an idea gets from a source through a medium to an audience. Furthermore, theory permits directing messages toward specific goals and predicting effects.

The concepts underlying mass communication theory can be mastered but they cannot be reduced to a pure science. Because of the nature of mass man, reporters must be prepared for messages to be misinterpreted and being aware of the problem develop backstops in message sending. Let us turn to three basic psychological factors that operate to contribute to the misinformation.

Factors Affecting Interpretation of Media Messages

Mass man has been described as rational yet lethargic, obstinate and rational. In each instance, the writer refers to mass man's ability to assimilate information on social, political and economic issues. The news writer researches a topic fully and builds what he thinks is a solid commonness with his audience only to discover that the receiver misinterprets the message. How can such a thing happen in the midst of such a plentiful information flow? Psychological theory presents three concepts that can contribute to the receiver's misunderstanding: selective exposure, selective perception and selective retention.

Selective exposure simply stated means that we tend to select media and messages that are consistent with our philosophies and attitudes. Under the concept of selective exposure, mass man ignores information with which he disagrees, and thus he can be misinformed even if the reporter successfully covers every angle to an event.

Selective perception is defined as an individual's interpretation of a specific message. The reader/viewer/listener may receive a message exactly as sent by the reporter yet come away with inaccurate information because his frame of reference leads him to interpret the message with prejudice.

Selective retention can result in misinformation because the reader/listener/viewer reads or hears the message as it was sent but remembers only certain portions–those that he agrees with.

Exercises: Chapter 1

Subject: Analysis of Content of a Daily Newspaper.

    1. Read one issue of a daily newspaper in your city or area and clip 2 examples of each of the following items: column of comment; editorial; advice column; hard news stories; soft news stories; attribution in news stories; and an interpretative article.

    2. Clip and mount the examples on regular typing paper and explain each briefly.

    3. Interview yourself and write a one-page news story. Do not write in the first person. Role play by assuming that you are a reporter interviewing another person. The material reported in the story must be factual. Write the story so that you communicate key or most important information about yourself to an impersonal mass audience.

    4. Read a daily newspaper (evening edition); listen to a local TV newscast (6 or 10 p.m.). Compare the play given by the two media by contrasting the news emphasis given to the top five stories on page one of the newspaper and the top three to five stories on the newscast. Now, write a one-page summary of your findings. Use news copy format.

2

What Is News?

One important function of mass media is to provide news and information. The news media–primarily newspapers, television, radio and newsmagazines–in carrying out this function give the American citizens a wide variety of news.

The question of what is news has shifted from a spot, event-centered definition to a broader one that includes interpretation and analysis. Most media experts agree that a broader definition is needed to keep the citizens informed.

For the beginning news writer, however, it is useful to consider some of the traditional commonalities that characterize news. The major characteristics are timeliness, proximity, prominence, impact and human interest. They form the bases or criteria that reporters and editors use to determine what is news–and they are useful in helping a news writer decide which elements go into a news story.

It is wise to remember that there is no universally accepted definition of news, but the following characteristics have been useful in the selection and writing of news.

Timeliness

A basic ingredient of news is timeliness. Readers, viewers and listeners expect and demand that news stories deal with current events, situations and trends. What is timely depends somewhat on the news medium. For a weekly newspaper, a timely story could be anything within one week; for a daily newspaper, it could mean anything within the past 24 hours, and for radio and television, it might be anything within hours, or since the last newscast which might have been within minutes.

Editors tell reporters to get new developments, to follow up and to update their stories. In other words, they are seeking to add the element of timeliness to news reports. Timeliness is usually a major ingredient in all news stories.

Proximity

This characteristic of news is generally defined as events, persons or institutions in the immediate coverage area, such as in the major circulation area for a newspaper or viewing or listening area for broadcasting. News consumers have a strong interest in local stories. They demand and expect to know what is happening in their community. The news media tend to look for proximity—or the local angle—in state, national and international stories because they know their customers expect it.

A strong local angle is not present in all news stories, but it is a characteristic that can help define what is considered newsworthy. For example, a story about a murder in New York City might not be news in a tiny Oklahoma town, but a murder in that small town would probably make Page One of the local newspaper. Proximity, therefore, is one of the common yardsticks by which news editors and reporters measure news.

Prominence

It is almost a cliche to repeat an old newsroom saying: names make news. But it is true—and the better known the name, the bigger the news. Another adage—some people are more newsworthy than others—is certainly true. Prominence can result from a variety of circumstances—positions in society, titles, past achievements, past publicity, for example. For whatever the reason, some individuals are high in prominence, and they make news wherever they go and whatever they do. The president of the United States is an example of a person who is extremely high in the news value of prominence. No matter what he does—significant or not—it is news. Celebrities, movie stars, athletes and others are often high in prominence.

Organizations, institutions and places may also be characterized as prominent. Large cities such as New York and Chicago are considered more newsworthy than smaller towns. Prominence can be the main news characteristic in a news story about a famous movie actress who breaks her big toe, for example. More often, prominence is combined with other news characteristics.

Impact

The characteristic of impact helps form the most important news stories. Impact is usually defined as anything that affects or will affect a large number of persons in a community. The effect can be direct or indirect. Stories that contain impact involve political, economic, social and moral consequences. This is the element most involved in hard news stories—and it is the main characteristic of the top stories of the day.

Stories involving taxes and economic developments, for example, are high in impact and are often played on Page One because they directly affect many people. Impact can be combined with proximity in stories about politics, school issues, city council actions, for instance, to form important local stories. National and international stories—often involving far-reaching issues such as war and peace—are high in impact because of concerns by media users. Today the world has shrunk so that events in foreign countries often have direct and immediate importance for American citizens. The energy crisis and oil shortages resulted from actions in other countries—and the consequences were felt in every American home. The interest in such stories is high.

Mass media writers must be alert for the impact angle in news writing. Obviously not all stories contain impact, but where it is present the writer must not downplay it.

Human Interest

Human interest is a broad category of news defined as anything of interest to humans. This characteristic covers all of the multitude of events, situations and trends that cannot be classified as straight news.

There is practically no limit to the kinds of things that could be called human interest. Conflict is one human interest element that might involve verbal or physical clashes between people, groups, nations or between man and nature. Crime, accidents and sports stories are examples of conflict.

Oddity is another type of human interest story. Oddity involves action or events rarer that just the unusual because most news stories are unusual. The oddity story has a twist or turn of events different from what is expected or predicted. An example of oddity would be the story about the recluse who lives and dies in poverty and leaves an estate worth several million dollars.

Children, animals or colorful personalities are often subjects for human interest stories. These stories have universal appeal and often score highest on readership surveys. The interest can be humor or pathos and can cause the reader or viewer to feel happy or sad. Humor can be an element in human interest. Humans are interested in the funny things that happen to people. The news writer must recognize the human interest angle in an item that might not possess the other news characteristics.

Combinations of Characteristics

The news characteristics described above do not occur in isolation. They are frequently mixed in varying degrees in the same story, and the news writer must decide which ones to emphasize. As mentioned earlier, almost all news stories contain timeliness—or the appearance of timeliness in the use of a word like "recently" or use of the present tense to convey immediacy. Most broadcast news copy uses present tense as do many newspaper headlines.

The other elements are often combined in stories. Top stories involved impact and often include proximity and prominence and occasionally some aspect of human interest such as conflict or oddity. Prominence and human interest are frequently combined in personality features or stories about celebrities and other well-known persons.

Exercises: Chapter 2

I. Which news characteristic is most appropriate for the following statements:

1. Well-known rock star steps off curb, twists ankle and ends up in hospital.
2. Mournful dog refuses to leave the grave of his master.
3. An event occurs within the circulation area of a newspaper or within the broadcast area of a TV or radio station.
4. The City Council approves a major street repair project which will mean a sharp increase in property taxes.
5. An editor tells a reporter to bring a story up-to-date with the latest development.

II. Find examples of stories in a newspaper that contain the news characteristics of timeliness, proximity, prominence, impact and human interest. Clip the stories, paste them on 8½ x 11 sheets and identify the news characteristics. Bring them to class for discussion.

III. In the following examples which single news characteristic--other than timeliness--makes the item newsworthy.

1. The state will lose two of its congressional seats on the basis of preliminary census figures released today.
2. A plan to increase fees for state auto license tags for next year by an average of $20 per tag was approved today.
3. A California man was killed today in a head-on collision five miles east of Dallas on Interstate 30.
4. Mickey Mantle, former New York Yankee baseball great, will be a special guest at a program Friday in his hometown of Commerce, Okla.
5. A cold-blooded character put the bite on detective Raymond Williams today when he searched a suspect. A baby alligator in the suspect's pocket nipped Williams on the finger.

6. Bert James, a former U.S. Senator, has taken a job as a political science professor at Arizona State University.

IV. Which two news characteristics—other than timeliness make the item newsworthy?

1. Local schools are scheduled to receive approximatately $1 million in state aid during the coming year.

2. Gov. Peter Carlson was a delighted golfer today. He made a 220-yard hole-in-one while playing in a pro-am tournament.

V. The following examples contain several news characteristics in addition to timeliness. Please list all you can identify. Indicate which single characteristic contributes most to making the item newsworthy.

1. Gov. David Brown and state Sen. Bill Dixon emerged as leaders in the state Democratic gubernatorial primary Tuesday and will meet in a runoff. Both candidates predicted victory. Brown led the balloting, but could not capture a majority.

2. An electrical power blackout hit large sections of the state today. Electrical company officials said the shortage was caused by a heavy accumulation of dead cockroaches in a key power transformer near Clarksville. Gov. David Brown said his office was investigating the situation.

3

News Story Structure

Inverted Pyramid

The beginning mass media writer must become familiar with principles of the basic news story structure commonly referred to as the inverted pyramid. The inverted pyramid, defined in a nutshell, simply means to place the most important information first in the story. Other paragraphs are arranged in descending order of importance. This structure is called the inverted pyramid because the conceptualized shape of such a story looks like the diagram on page 16.

A word of caution should be expressed. This form is only a blueprint to be used as a general guide. It is not a rigid straitjacket, and it permits flexibility in writing structure. The inverted pyramid form is used for straight news when the main purpose is to convey factual information quickly to a reader, viewer or listener. Most spot news stories are written in this manner.

Technological and historical changes helped to develop the inverted pyramid. The rise of a mass audience for news in the 19th century led to structuring news for quick reading. The telegraph was used for sending news stories, especially important fast-breaking ones such as battles during the Civil War. News sent over telegraph wires had to get to the point quickly because wire time was expensive. The long leisurely constructed essay and literary-style writing popular in an earlier time were not suitable for the new mass medium.

The structure serves four functions. First, and foremost, the structure helps the reader. It enables him to scan a story, read only one or two paragraphs and get the gist of the news. A reader can decide if he wants to read more of the story; he can stop anywhere in the story and know that he has read the most important elements. In other words, he doesn't have to read the entire story to get the main points.

The average issue of a daily newspaper contains as many words as a

Diagram: Inverted Pyramid

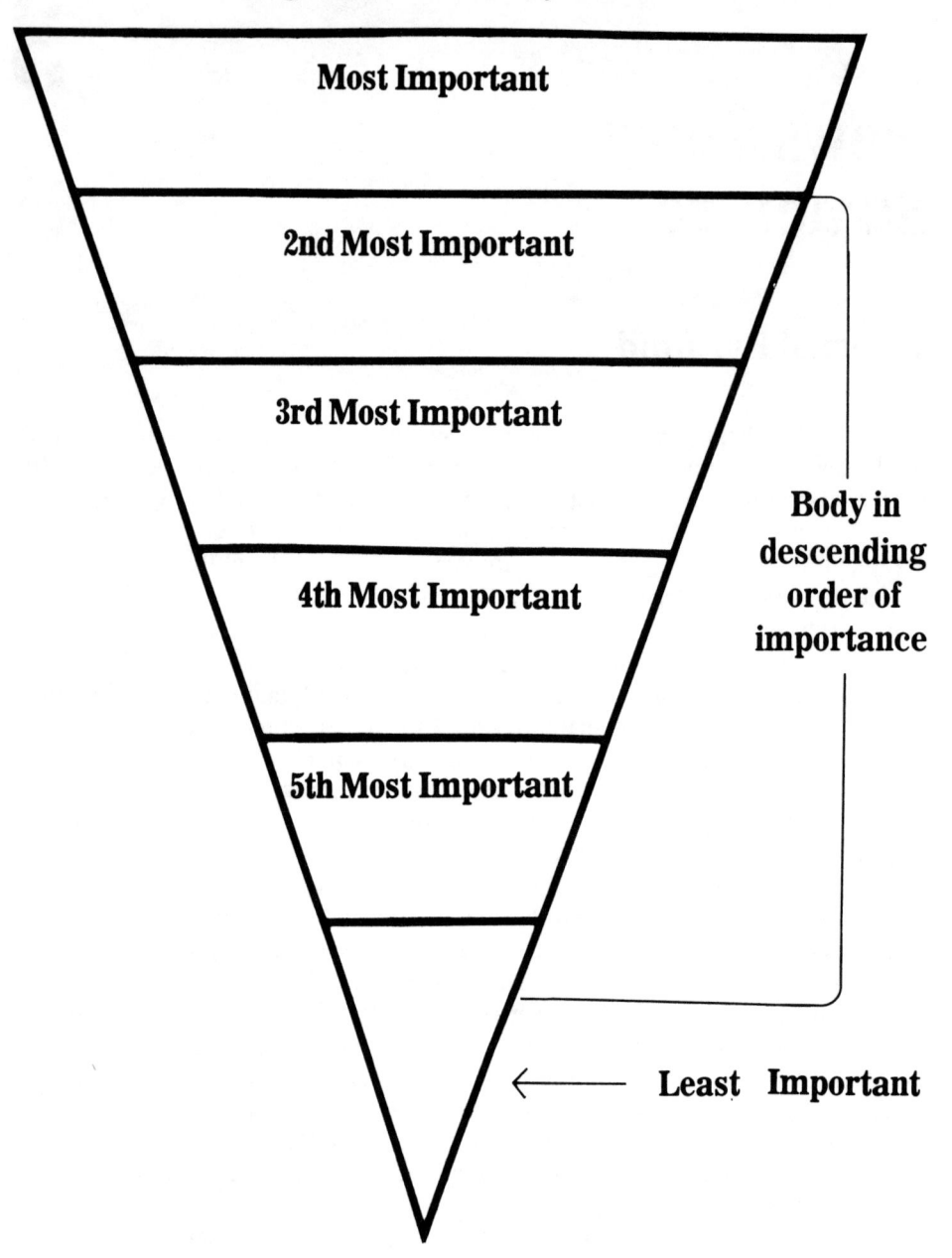

- Most Important
- 2nd Most Important
- 3rd Most Important
- 4th Most Important
- 5th Most Important

} Body in descending order of importance

← Least Important

full-length book. Most readers spend 30 minutes or less reading the newspaper. Therefore, they must scan many stories. The inverted pyramid enables them to do so.

Second, the structure enables the editor to cut a story from the bottom. The story does not have to be rewritten to fit a smaller space. The modern newspaper could not be produced without this time-saving function of the inverted pyramid. Wire stories and local news stories are processed within a short time. Often there is a deadline of only a few minutes to write and edit a news story. The story can also be expanded quickly by adding material at the bottom.

A third important function of the inverted pyramid is to help the headline writer. This function is related to the one mentioned above because this is another way the form assists the editing process. The headline can be written from the first paragraphs of the story, and the copy editor can get the essentials quickly without having to read the entire story.

A fourth function of the inverted pyramid is to assist the reporter when he writes a straight news story. The reporter can quickly compose his story using this organizational pattern. For an experienced reporter, the process can become automatic. The beginning writer needs practice to develop the ability to write a story using the inverted pyramid. The four functions listed here are the major reasons for the usefulness of the inverted pyramid for both print and broadcast.

The following is an example of a news story written in the inverted pyramid form:

>HOUSTON (AP)--A Michigan electrician who received a heart and two lungs died today shortly after completion of the multiple transplant operation, a hospital spokeswoman said.
>Douglas Granger, 45, of Coldwater, Mich., underwent the four-hour operation to correct a severe lung disease diagnosed a year ago.
>Granger died from "bleeding complications throughout the chest" about 20 minutes after Dr. Denton Cooley and a team of surgeons finished the surgery, said Hazel Haby, spokeswoman for the Texas Heart Institute at St. Luke's Hospital.
>Granger was the third heart-lung patient to die here within the past two months. **(Used by permission of The Associated Press.)**

The lead is a summary answering the questions a reader wants to know about the story. The other paragraphs are arranged in descending order of importance, allowing the story to be cut from the bottom if necessary. The lead paragraph could stand alone because it is complete and communicates the gist of the story. Notice how the next three paragraphs add to and elaborate on information in the lead.

Here is another example of an inverted pyramid lead:

> TULSA (UPI)—A bogus supply company set up by the FBI that authorities say paid kickbacks to county commissioners in Oklahoma figured prominently in the indictments of two Pawnee County commissioners, officials said Wednesday.
>
> The FBI supply story, termed a "sting operation" by first assistant U.S. Atty. Ben Baker, marked the first time the FBI had used the tactic in the Northern Judicial District during the county commissioner kickback investigation.
>
> The federal grand jury indictment named two Commissioners. One was accused of 17 counts of mail fraud and one was accused of 25 mail fraud counts. . . .
> (Used by permission of United Press International.)

The inverted pyramid form is the basic story structure, but other forms are commonly used. Two of these are chronological order and suspended interest. These forms are similar and have been used for years on feature stories. In recent years, they have been used with indepth stories dealing with serious news-related topics. They are still popular ways to organize the light, off-beat human interest story.

Chronological Order

When an action sequence or a series of related events are involved, chronological order is often used as the structure for the story or a portion of it. Frequently such a story will have a summary lead and then move into a chronological order account.

Note how the story below has a summary lead which is followed by a step-by-step chronological order telling of what happened.

> Police were looking today for a robber who was so nervous he shot himself in the hand and escaped with no money.
>
> A man, described as about 20 years old and

extremely nervous, entered a convenience store at 101 N. Main St. about noon today.

He pulled a gun from his coat pocket and demanded money from the cash register.

The clerk opened the register and laid some bills on the counter.

The man reached for the bills and the gun discharged, sending a bullet into his hand. He dropped the gun and the money and fled the scene.

Suspended Interest

The suspended interest format is often used to tell short, frequently humorous stories which have a twist or trick ending. The writer reverses the inverted pyramid and saves the punchline for the end. The story follows a narrative or chronological order, but unlike the chronological order there is no summary lead. The reader must read all of the story to find what happened. Here is an example of a suspended interest story:

Max Preston, 75, has lived in a one-room shack near a southside auto salvage yard for years.

Preston, who says the only mail he usually gets is his monthly Social Security check, stopped Friday to check his mail.

In his mail box he found his Social Security check. And a cashier's check for $5,000 with a note reading "Merry Christmas, Max."

The note was unsigned.

Summary Leads

The inverted pyramid has a summary lead which is often the first paragraph of the story, but it could include the first two or three paragraphs. The lead must give a quick, concise summary of the story. Many readers will read only the lead.

The news writer faces a difficult but important task in fashioning the lead. An understanding of the news characteristics will aid the writer in determining which information and angle should be in the lead.

In addition to the news characteristics, the news writer can be assisted by the 5 Ws and the H–who, what, when, where, why and how–long used by writers to select and organize facts. After a decision is made based on the news characteristics that the story is newsworthy, the writer must begin the organization of information

Who

The who and the what are often combined as the main focus of a lead. Many leads center on who did what, or what happened to whom. Often it is difficult to separate the two and many leads could be classified as who-what or what-who. A who lead begins with the person or persons being emphasized in the story. The identification is often in general terms, called the indefinite who, instead of by proper name. The proper name can be placed lower in the story which helps unclutter the lead. A typical lead:

> A Dallas policeman involved in the shooting of a fleeing robbery suspect last week was placed on administrative leave without pay today.

This lead places the emphasis on the Dallas policeman, the best identification to use in this case. His name can go lower in the story. The identification in the lead should be the most pertinent and newsworthy for the story. Any other identification would not be suitable, although other identifications can be used elsewhere in the story. In the example above, the policeman might be identified in a lower paragraph as the father of three.

When the name of the person or persons emphasized in the lead is well known to readers, the proper name can be used. For example:

> Mayor Tom Belden returned today after testifying before a Senate committee about financial problems faced by cities.

In this lead, the mayor's name is well known to the readers. An identification of "mayor" is still used with the name. A proper name standing alone in the lead might be meaningless to the reader.

What

Many news leads begin with what happened, or what is going to happen. In spot news stories such as accidents, fires and crimes, the emphasis should be on the event. In a news story with several "whats", the news writer sometimes has a tough job deciding what the story is about, and what to feature in the lead. With multiple whats, the writer usually is well advised to select the top two or three and use summarization. Here is an example of a what lead:

> A fire believed to have been started by arsonists destroyed three businesses in a South Side shopping center early today.

As mentioned earlier, the who and the what are often mixed. The who and the what are inseparable in many stories. The following lead combines the two:

> Two 18-year-old men were indicted Thursday by a federal grand jury in Austin on charges of counterfeiting $1 bills.

When

The when and the where are usually in a secondary position in the lead. The lead more often stresses the who-what angle. Seldom will the when or the where be used first. Here is an example of a lead that emphasizes when:

> Thursday is the deadline for candidates to file for the City Council election scheduled Nov. 3.

More often the when is placed in an inconspicuous spot, frequently after the major verb. Like this:

> The City Council voted Thursday to increase the garbage pickup fee by $1 for each residential customer.

Since timeliness is one of the characteristics of news, the when element is important and should be high in the story, but rarely is it first.

Where

The where is another key element for lead writing. Proximity is one of the characteristics of news which makes where the story occurred important.

Seldom, however, is the where the most newsworthy feature. It is usually subordinate in the lead. This lead emphasizes the where:

>Memorial Stadium will be expanded to 20,000 seats under a plan approved Saturday by university regents.

The where is more often placed lower in the lead like this:

>An Oklahoma man wanted for murder was arrested in Beaumont Thursday by Texas law enforcement officers.

A dateline is used on stories that originate outside the newspaper home area. The dateline tells the reader where the event occurred.

>FORT WORTH--U.S. District Judge William Owens granted a stay of execution today for a convicted killer scheduled to die Friday in Huntsville.

For local stories, the specific city is sometimes not necessary because the reader will understand that it is the local community. For example:

>A study committee recommended today that a city sales tax of one-half of one cent be approved to fund a public transportation authority.

Why or How

The why of a story refers to the cause or reason behind an event's occurrence. The how deals with how something happened. These two elements are generally secondary to the other Ws in spot news stories. The why and the how are important elements for interpretative, analysis and depth stories. The why and the how might be featured occasionally in a straight news lead. Here is an example of a why lead:

>In an attempt to raise funds for a mass transit system, the City Council today appointed a committee to draft plans for a sales tax increase.

A how lead will center on the means by which something happened:

> A loose wire which caused an electrical short was blamed for a fire that destroyed a $100,000 home here early today.

Unity

Writers must pay special attention to transition within the body of an inverted pyramid story. The lead summarizes the essentials which reverses the normal order of story-telling. A story told in chronological order allows the writer to introduce details in a sequential pattern which gives the story a natural flow from one element to the next.

The inverted pyramid interrupts this natural flow, and an extra effort must be made to achieve unity. The paragraphs must be tied together in some functional way; there must be a relationship between the paragraphs to move the reader through the story. Lower paragraphs add more details to the story, and the reader's thoughts should be directed by adding information that could be expected to follow logically.

One common device is to use an indefinite identification in the lead and to put the proper name or names and other details lower, perhaps in the second paragraph. Here is an example:

> A 66-year-old Dallas woman died early today in a fire which destroyed her small frame home.
> Mrs. William Peters, who lived at 2050 N. Willow St., perished in the blaze which began...

The added identification of the proper name and address are expected by the reader and provide a functional link to the lead. One obvious way to achieve unity is through use of words such as **however, meanwhile, therefore, except, also, but, earlier, because** and other transitional terms. Here's an example of linkage words used to introduce new paragraphs:

> The Smithfield City Council voted Tuesday to fire three members of the city's 11-member police department.
> **Earlier,** Police Chief Matt Jones said he had lost confidence in the performance of the officers.
> **However,** the chief did not appear at the council meeting when the vote was taken to dismiss the three.

An effective technique for achieving transition through the body of a straight news story is to repeat key words. In the following example notice how the word **horses** is repeated in several paragraphs. Also transition is achieved with use of "meanwhile" to begin the second paragraph and "last week" at the start of the third paragraph.

> TYLER, Texas (UPI)--More than 500 people applied to adopt **wild horses** that were victims of what a humane organization called the "worst case of abuse" in the history of the government's adoptive program, officials said Wednesday.
>
> Meanwhile, the organization--the American Horse-Protection Association--filed suit in Washington against the U.S. Interior Department seeking an injunction against more large-scale transfers of **wild horses** to private owners and a revamped screening process.
>
> Last week authorities discovered starving **horses** packed in a small pasture enclosure near Pittsburg in East Texas.
>
> When they were discovered, 39 **horses** had died and others, including a number of colts, were near death because of exposure and malnutrition.
>
> More than 500 applicants for **horses** participated in a lottery for the horses in Tyler. The **horses** will be given to owners in the order of their lottery selection and following strict screening procedures. (**Used by permission of United Press International.**)

Transition can be gained through use of linkage phrases also. Here is an example:

> The county commissioners adopted a plan Wednesday calling for construction of a 400-space parking garage in the Wedgewood area.
>
> In other action, the commissioners...

Multi-Dimensional

A longer more complicated story with several key angles and developments poses a difficult challenge for the writer. The basic story structure is still inverted pyramid, but transition from topic to topic is more complex.

One rule followed by some news writers is to present no new material after the half-way point. The writer presents main points in the top of the story and returns to each topic to fill in details lower down. If all information is presented about a single topic before going on to the next, some key elements could be too low in the story. The preference is to give a short summary of each point high in the story and return to that topic for more details. The writer can then discuss topics at length. Transition is clear because the subjects were mentioned at the beginning of the story. There are no jarring surprises for the reader. The following lead has several elements:

> The county commissioners decided Tuesday to cut expenditures by 1 percent, to hold salary increases to 3 percent and to reduce the amount of money carried over to the next fiscal year.

There are three elements summarized in the lead. The details for these topics can be introduced lower in the story. An outline of the structure of this story would look like the diagram on page 26.

Diagram: Straight News Story

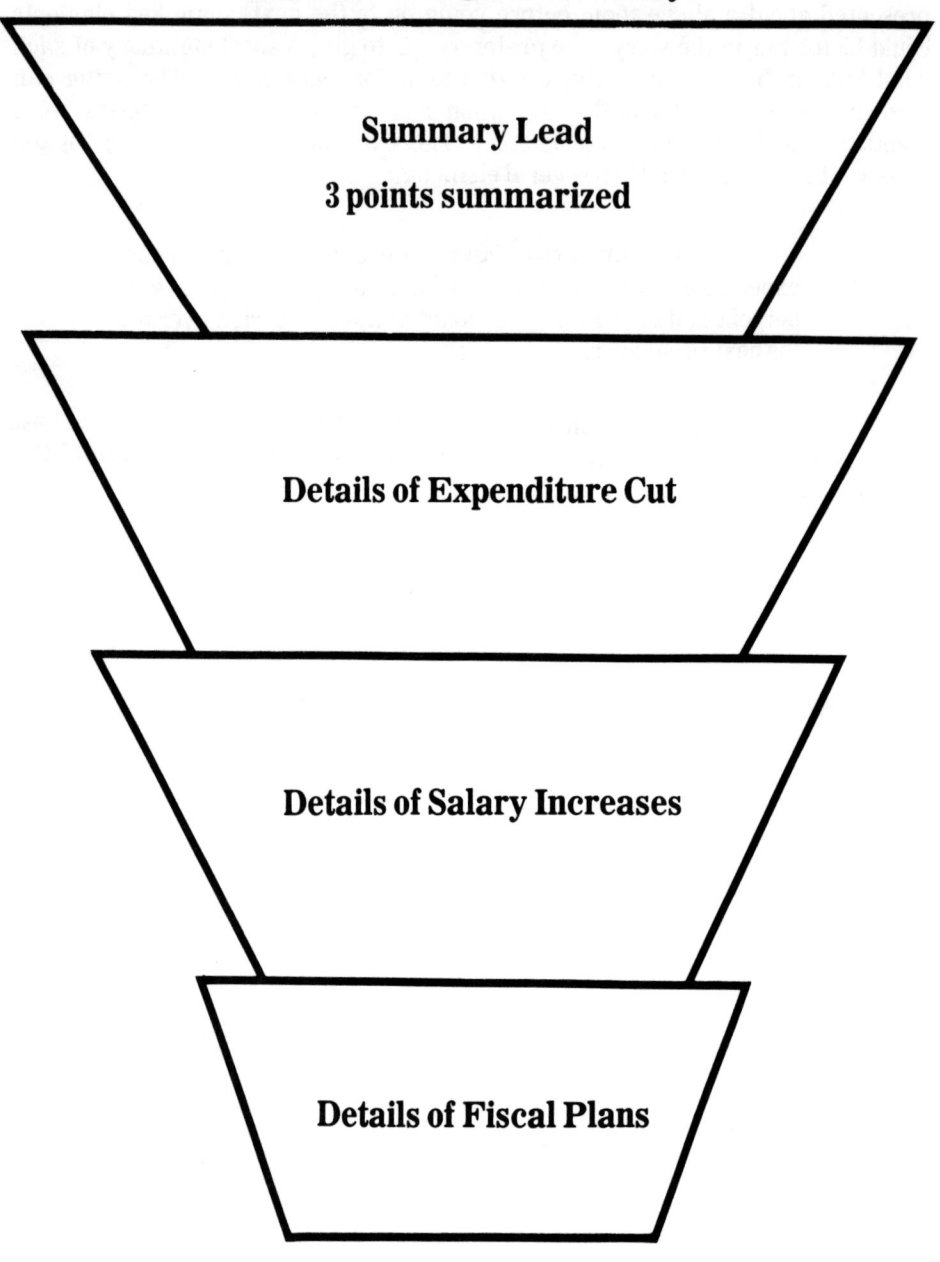

Summary Lead

3 points summarized

Details of Expenditure Cut

Details of Salary Increases

Details of Fiscal Plans

Exercises: Chapter 3

I. Write summary lead paragraphs from the following facts:

1. City Council members are concerned about apartment construction near the Municipal Airport. Airplanes landing and taking off from the airport create noise. Sound experts say the apartments are being built in areas with noise levels of 60 to 70 decibels. The council Thursday will consider an ordinance to require soundproofing to reduce the noise levels to 45 decibels inside the apartments.

2. Perry Sanders, 45 years of age, works as a janitor at Reed Jewelry Store, 101 North Main Street. Sanders was working at the store late last night when he heard a noise. He went to the front of the store where he saw a man trying to break into the store. Sanders tripped the burglar alarm, ran out the door and tackled the man. When police arrived, Sanders was holding the man down. Police said the suspect will be charged with attempted burglary.

3. Write a complete story of four or five paragraphs from the following information:

—At a Central Turnpike toll booth; toll booth located in northern part of the city at intersection of Central Turnpike and State Highway 80.

—A tractor-trailer truck driven by John P. Barton, 35, of Okmulgee, Okla. Accident occurred at 2:15 p.m. Truck failed to stop at toll booth and plowed into five cars waiting at the toll booth.

—Six people in the cars were killed and three were critically injured. Driver of the truck was also killed. Crash caused an explosion and fire. Identification of victims not known at this time. Crash scattered debris across five lanes of the highway. Victims were burned beyond recognition in the fire which destroyed the cars. Police said they did not know what caused the accident and why the truck did not stop at the toll booth.

4. Write a complete story from the following facts:

The Pinewood Baptist Church has a project to help church work in Honduras and El Salvador. The Pinewood congregation became interested when it learned of the plight of poverty-stricken people in those countries. The church, under the direction of Reverend Bill Jones, pastor of the 1200-member church, began a drive to send Spanish-language Bibles and well-drilling equipment to the area. The church today finished packing 10,000 Spanish-language Bibles and $100,000 worth of water well drilling equipment. The supplies will be sent by airplane next week to three church missions in Honduras and El Salvador. Jones and eight Pinewood Church members will travel with the supplies to the three missions.

5. Write a complete story from the following facts:

About 2 a.m. today some turbulent weather developed in the area and a line of storms moved across the city from the southwest to the northeast. Wind gusts up to 60 miles an hour were reported. Rainfall amounted to about three inches in some parts of the city. The storms moved at about 20 miles per hour and were out of the city by 4 a.m. A tree was struck by lightning and fell on a house at 2022 Elm Street but there were no injuries. About a hundred homes on the south side of town were without electricity for one hour. There were reports of some small hail. A tornado watch was in effect during the storm, but no funnel clouds were sighted. A few streets were temporarily closed by high water for a short time.

6. Write a complete story from the following facts:

An election was held today on a proposal to build a rail transit system in the city. The proposal was for one hundred million dollars to construct a 30 mile rail project to link the downtown area with the suburbs. Also included in the plan were satellite parking lots and transit terminals. The proposal was defeated by city voters 65,320 to 40,309. Transit Authority Director Max Allen said the rail transit plan is the best way to solve the traffic congestion problem in the downtown area. He said the defeat is a serious blow, but he said he had hopes the plan could be revised and brought before the voters again in a year or two. Only about 20 percent of eligible voters cast ballots on the proposal.

7. Write a complete story from the following facts:

A study by the Lone Star Research Association of Austin, Texas, was released today. The study contained the following information: Energy use in the residential sector would decline in the next 10 years, but the use by industry would increase. Consumers will be unable to afford heating and cooling practices of earlier years because the price of electricity and natural gas will increase. Ten years ago 85 percent of the U.S. population lived at 70 degrees or above in the winter, but today that figure had dropped to 50 percent. Conservation by American homeowners has led to a 20 percent drop in residential use in the last ten years. More Americans are using wood stoves, portable heaters and other devices for heating.

8. Write a complete story from the following facts:

The zoning and planning Commission held a meeting at 8 P.M. last night in City Hall. About 50 people attended the meeting which lasted until 11 p.m. Planning Commission chairman Richard Morgan called the meeting to order and said the main business was consideration of a proposal to limit high-density multifamily apartments in the city. Commissioner William Joyce said limits on future apartment growth would reduce the work force needed by new industry in the city. Commissioner Ken James said the city had plenty of apartments. He said a request for rezoning for apartments on 425 acres in the southern part of the city should be denied. A lengthy debate followed on the apartment issue. The commission voted 4 to 1 against a moratorium on future apartments in the city and delayed a decision on the 425 acres.

4

Refining the News Story

Sentence Structure

Mass media writing is aimed at the widest possible audience for a publication or broadcast station. To cater to a diversified audience, media writers use simple, direct, clear, concise and vigorous language. It is altered for special-interest magazines and other publications and broadcasts for smaller groups.

The standard for journalism and media writing is the simple declarative sentence, packed with information-laden nouns and verbs. The simple sentence can be varied with compound and complex sentences to add interest and emphasis and to prevent monotony. Phrases, clauses, modifiers and other elements are used when necessary to add to the basic statement contained in the sentence.

One idea per sentence is a good rule for media writers. Some publications frequently use one sentence per paragraph. These techniques differ from those taught in English composition classes where longer paragraphs and longer sentences are acceptable because the messages are directed to an audience that has more leisure time to digest information.

Shorter sentences and paragraphs are demanded in the media because they are easier to change in a breaking news story. The simple English sentence has subjects first, verbs second and objects third. Readers and listeners are familiar with this structure; therefore, it conveys meaning to them quickly and easily. For example: **A tornado (subject) hit (verb) the city (object).**

This structure places the emphasis on what happened and does it first in the sentence. The word order is important to achieve clarity. The active voice is preferred in mass media writing, except in sentences where the emphasis is on the object. The example above could be put in the passive voice like this: **The** city was hit by the tornado. (passive).

This construction is used when the writer wants to place emphasis on "the city." Passive voice leads to non-emphatic statements that lack interest and vigor. Too many passive voice sentences will bore the reader or listener. News stories consisting solely of simple sentences soon become monotonous. The basic structure needs to be varied by adding modifiers, phrases and clauses. Compound and complex sentences can be used.

The media writer needs to understand the principle of subordination to make these more complex structures work. The reader or listener must grasp the main idea easily, and the relationship of minor elements to this must be clear.

Troubled writing results when the writer does not follow this concept. Muddled, confused and illogical sentences result. Sentences that begin with phrases or clauses can cause problems because misplaced emphasis can get in the way of meaning. A phrase or clause should be used to introduce a sentence only when it is important. Here's an example: **During the night, a tornado hit the city.** The example begins with a phrase. In most cases this phrase should go later in the sentence, such as, **A tornado hit the city during the night.**

The subject is usually the most important element and is placed first. This word order should be changed only when a more important element goes first.

Compound and complex sentences should be used to break the monotony of simple sentences and to add flow and rhythm to a story. But they should be used only when combining closely related elements, such as: **Six people died when a tornado hit the city during the night.**

Modifiers

Modifiers can cause problems for media writers. Adjectives are shunned or used sparingly because of connotative and imprecise meanings. Adverbs often can be eliminated because they add nothing to the meaning already carried by the verb. Modifiers are sometimes necessary, but they often clutter sentences. That is why they must be handled with care.

A good writing rule is to let the facts speak for themselves. Writers get into trouble when they try to embellish a story with unneeded modifiers. A modifier would be out of place in this example: **Six people died when a deadly tornado struck the city during the night.** The word "deadly" adds nothing but clutter to the sentence.

A general rule is that modifiers should be as close as possible to the words they modify. Meaning is not clear when they are widely separated. Such construction can lead to misplaced or dangling modifiers which are often humorous to readers and critics but embarrassing to the writer. For example, **Running down the street, a house was seen by the man.** The phrase that introduces the sentence should be followed by the subject.

Parallel Construction

Another problem is caused by lack of parallel construction. The same grammatical forms and parts of speech should be used in a sentence. For example, **He likes to run, to swim and hunt.** The same form should be used throughout: "to hunt" would be correct.

Common Mistakes

The Associated Press Managing Editors Association has compiled a list of 50 common writing mistakes. This list is included here as a guide to prevent frequent mistakes:

1. Affect, effect. Generally, affect is the verb; effect is the noun. "The letter did not affect the outcome." "The letter had a significant effect." But effect is also a verb meaning to bring about. Thus: "It is almost impossible to effect change."
2. Afterward, afterwards. Use afterward. The dictionary allows use of afterwards only as a second form. The same thinking applies to toward and towards. Use toward.
3. All right. That's the way to spell it. The dictionary may list alright as a legitimate word but it is not acceptable in standard usage, says Random House.
4. Allude, elude. You allude to (or mention) a book. You elude (or escape) a pursuer.
5. Annual. Don't use first with it. If it's the first time, it can't be annual.
6. Averse, adverse: If you don't like something, you are averse (or opposed) to it. Adverse is an adjective: adverse (bad) weather, adverse conditions.
7. Block, bloc: A block is a coalition of persons or a group with the same purpose or goal. Don't call it a

block, which has some 40 dictionary definitions.

8. Compose, comprise: Remember that you compose things by putting them together. Once the parts are put together, the object comprises or includes or embraces the parts.

9. Couple of. You need the of. It's never "a couple tomatoes."

10. Demolish, destroy. They mean to do away with completely. You can't partially demolish or destroy something, nor is there any need to say totally destroyed.

11. Different from. Things and people are different from each other. Don't write that they are different than each other.

12. Drown. Don't say someone was drowned unless an assailant held the victim's head under water. Just say the victim drowned.

13. Due to, owing to, because of: We prefer the last.

Wrong: The game was canceled due to rain.
Stilted: Owing to rain, the game was canceled.
Right: The game was canceled because of rain.

14. Ecology, environment. They are not synonymous. Ecology is the study of the relationship between organisms and their environment.

Right: The laboratory is studying the ecology of man and the desert.
Right: There is much interest in animal ecology these days.
Wrong: Even so simple an undertaking as maintaining a lawn affects ecology.
Right: Even so simple an undertaking as maintaining a lawn affects our environment.

15. Either: It means one or the other, not both.

Wrong: There were lions on either side of the door.
Right: There were lions on each side of the door.

16. Fliers, flyers. Airmen are fliers. Handbills are flyers.

17. Flout, flaunt. They aren't the same words; they mean completely different things and they're very

commonly confused.

Flout means to mock, to scoff or to show disdain for.

Flaunt means to display ostentatiously.

18. Funeral service. A redundant expression. A funeral is a service.

19. Head up. People don't head up committees. They head them.

20. Hopefully. One of the most commonly misused words, in spite of what the dictionary may say. Hopefully should describe the way the subject feels. For instance:

Hopefully, I shall present the plan to the president. (This means I will be hopeful when I do it.)

But it is something else again when you attribute hope to a nonperson. You may write: Hopefully, the war will end soon. This means you hope the war will end soon, but it is not what you are writing. What you mean is: I hope the war will end soon.

21. Imply and infer. The speaker implies. The hearer infers.

22. In advance of, prior to. Use before; it sounds natural.

23, It's, its. Its is the possessive, it's is the contraction of it is.

Wrong: What is it's name?
Right: What is its name? Its name is Fido.
Right: It's the first time he's scored tonight.
Right: It's my coat.

24. Lay, lie. Lay is the action word; lie is the state of being.

Wrong: The body will lay in state until Wednesday.
Right: The body will lie in state until Wednesday.

However, the past tense of lie is lay.

Right: The body lay in state from Tuesday until Wednesday.
Wrong: the body laid in state from Tuesday until Wednesday.

The past participle and the plain past tense of lay is laid.

Right: He laid the pencil on the pad.

Right: He had laid the pencil on the pad.
Right: The hen laid an egg.

25. Leave, let: Leave alone means to depart from or cause to be in solitude. Let alone means to be undisturbed.

Wrong: The man had pulled a gun on her, but Mr. Jones intervened and talked him into leaving her alone.

Right: The man had pulled a gun on her, but Mr. Jones intervened and talked him into letting her alone.

Right: When I entered the room I saw that Jim and Mary were sleeping, so I decided to leave them alone.

26. Less, Fewer. If you can separate items in the quantities being compared, use fewer. If not, use less.

Wrong: The Rams are inferior to the Vikings because they have less good linemen.

Right: The Rams are inferior to the Vikings because they have fewer good linemen.

Right: The Rams are inferior to the Vikings because they have less experience.

27. Like, as. Don't use like for as or as if. In general, use like to compare with nouns, pronouns; use as when comparing with phrases and clauses that contain a verb.

Wrong: Jim blocks the linebacker like he should.

Right: Jim blocks the linebacker as he should.

Right: Jim blocks like a pro.

28. Marshall, marshal. Generally, the first form is correct only when the word is a proper noun: John Marshall. The second form is the verb form: Marilyn will marshal her forces. And the second form is the one to use for a title: Fire Marshal Stan Anderson, Field Marshal Erwin Rommel.

29. Mean, average, median: Use mean as synonymous with average. Each word refers to the sum of all components divided by the number of components. Median is the number that has as many components above it as below it.

30. Nouns. There's a growing trend toward using them as verbs. Resist it. Host, headquarters and author,

for instance, are nouns, even though the dictionary may acknowledge they can be used as verbs. If you do, you'll come up with a monstrosity like: "Headquartered at his country home, John Doe hosted a party to celebrate the book he had authored."

31. Oral, verbal: Use oral when use of the mouth is central to the thought; the word emphasizes the idea of human utterance. Verbal may apply to spoken or written words; it connotes the process of reducing ideas to writing. Usually, it's a verbal contract, not an oral one, if it's in writing.

32. Over and more than. They aren't interchangeable. Over refers to spatial relationships. The plane flew over the city. More than is used with figures: In the crowd were more than 1,000 fans.

33. Parallel construction. Thoughts in series in the same sentence require parallel construction.

Wrong: The union delivered demands for an increase of 10 percent in wages and to cut the work week to 30 hours.

Right: The union delivered demands for an increase of 10 percent in wages and for a reduction in the work week to 30 hours.

34. Peddle, pedal. When selling something, you peddle it. When riding a bicycle or similar form of locomotion, you pedal it.

35. Pretense, pretext: They're different, but it's a tough distinction. A pretext is that which is put forward to conceal a truth.

He was discharged for tardiness, but this was only a pretext for general incompetence.

A pretense is a "false show"; a more overt act intended to conceal personal feelings.

My profuse compliments were all pretense.

36. Principle, principal. A guiding rule or basic truth is a principle. The first, dominant, or leading thing is principal. Principle is a noun; principal may be a noun or an adjective.

Right: It's the principle of the thing.

Right: Liberty and justice are two principles on which our nation is founded.

Right: Hitting and fielding are the principal activities in baseball.

Right: Robert Jamieson is the school principal.

37. Redundancies to avoid: Easter Sunday. Make it Easter.

Incumbent Congressman. Congressman.

Owns his own home. Owns his home.

The company will close down. The company will close.

Jones, Smith, Johnson and Reid were all convicted. Jones, Smith, Johnson and Reid were convicted.

Jewish rabbi. Just rabbi.

8 p.m. tonight. All you need is 8 tonight or 8 p.m. today.

During the winter months. During the winter.

Both Reid and Jones were denied pardons. Reid and Jones were denied pardons.

I am currently tired. I am tired.

Autopsy to determine the cause of death. Autopsy.

38. Refute. The word connotes success in argument and almost always implies editorial judgment.

Wrong: Father Bury refuted the arguments of the pro-abortion faction.

Right: Father Bury responded to the arguments of the pro-abortion faction.

39. Reluctant, reticent. If he doesn't want to act, he is reluctant. If he doesn't want to speak, he is reticent.

40. Say, said. The most serviceable words in the journalist's language are the forms of the verb to say. Let a person say something, rather than declare or admit or point out. And never let him grin, smile, frown or giggle something.

41. Slang. Don't try to use "with-it" slang. Usually a term is on the way out by the time we get it in print.

Wrong: The police cleared the demonstrators with a sunrise bust.

42. Spelling. It's basic. If reporters can't spell and copy editors can't spell, we're in trouble. Some ripe ones for the top of your list:

It's consensus, not concensus.

It's restaurateur, not restauranteur.

It's dietitian, not dietician.

43. Temperatures. They may get higher or lower, but they don't get warmer or cooler.

Wrong: Temperatures are expected to warm up in the area Friday.

Right: Temperatures are expected to rise in the area Friday.

44. That, which. That tends to restrict the reader's thought and direct it the way you want it to go; which is nonrestrictive, introducing a bit of subsidiary information. For example:

The lawnmower that is in the garage needs sharpening. (Meaning: We have more than one lawnmower. The one in the garage needs sharpening.)

The lawnmower, which is in the garage, needs sharpening. (Meaning: Our lawnmower needs sharpening. It's in the garage.)

The statue that graces our entry hall is on loan from the museum. (Meaning: Of all the statues around here, the one in the entry hall is on loan.)

The statue, which graces our entry hall, is on loan. (Meaning: Our statue is on loan. It happens to be in the entry hall.)

Note that which clauses take commas, signaling they are not essential to the meaning of the sentence.

45. Under way, not underway. But don't say something got under way. Say it started or began.

46. Unique. Something that is unique is the only one of its kind. It can't be very unique or quite unique or somewhat unique or rather unique. Don't use it unless you really mean it.

47. Up. Don't use it as a verb.

Wrong: The manager said he would up the price next week.

Right: The manager said he would raise the price next week.

48. Who, whom. A tough one, but generally you're safe to use whom to refer to someone who has been the object of an action. Who is the word when the somebody has been the actor:

A 19-year-old woman, to whom the room was rented, left the window open.

A 19-year-old woman, who rented the room, left the window open.

49. Who's, whose. Though it incorporates an apostrophe, who's is not a possessive. It's a contraction for who is. Whose is the possessive.

Wrong: I don't know who's coat it is.
Right: I don't know whose coat it is.
Right: Find out who's there.

50. Would: be careful about using would when constructing a conditional past tense.

Wrong: If Soderholm would not have had an injured foot, Thompson wouldn't have been in the lineup.

Right: If Soderholm had not had an injured foot, Thompson wouldn't have been in the lineup. (**Used by permission of the APME.**)

Specificity and Conciseness

Media writers have to be specific and concise to attract and hold readers and listeners who have many other demands on their time. Specific concrete language with definite details and images is the surest way to hold an audience. Vague, general words and sentences should be shunned or rephrased to make them vivid.

Abstract words and sentences lack the specificity needed for media writing. For example, "animal" is more abstract than "goat" because the word "animal" includes many kinds. "Goat" narrows the meaning, making it more concrete for the reader or listener. Some words that refer to ideas, such as "democracy," "humanism" and "liberal," are more abstract. There is less agreement on the meaning of these words than on words such as "chair," "goat" and "pencil." Abstract words have to be used, but confusion and boredom are reduced for the readers and listeners if they are explained in concrete terms. For example:

The tall building was damaged in the storm. (vague)

The 20-story building was damaged in the storm. (better, more specific)

There were some sheep loose on the highway. (vague)

>   Twenty sheep were loose on the highway.
> (better)

Readers and listeners want specific, pertinent details that make a story come alive with information and meaning. They want to know exact sizes, weights, distances, colors, smells, numbers and other details. The specifics must not be tedious or unnecessary. The writer must select the appropriate ones that add to the story.

In addition to specific details, the media writer must strive to be concise. Unnecessary and unfamiliar words should be avoided. The general tendency toward wordiness is a barrier to understanding, and media writers have to battle continually to be concise. Governments, schools, businesses and other institutions contribute to wordiness with bureaucratic, bloated language. For example:

> The president announced the names of the winners. (wordy)
> The president identified the winners. (better)
> The dead body was found in the field. (wordy)
> The body was found in the field. (better)
> The consensus of opinion is that he will run again. (wordy)
> The consensus is that he will run again.

The examples above have needless words that add nothing to the meaning of the sentences. Most newsrooms have long lists of common expressions that are banned because they are wordy. The media writer can avoid problems with conciseness by developing a keen understanding of word meanings. Many wordiness problems are caused by writers who are not clear on the meaning of the words they use.

Handling Quotes

Media writers must quote sources. Most news stories, public relations releases, feature stories and even advertising copy involve the use of direct and indirect quotes. The writer must be skilled in their use.

Direct quotes are the exact words spoken by a source, and indirect quotes are paraphrases or summaries of what a source said. Direct quotes are always enclosed inside quote marks, with careful attention paid to placement and frequency of the attribution. For example:

> "I will run again," the mayor said. (Direct)
> The mayor said he would run again. (Indirect)

Both direct and indirect quotes are used heavily in news writing, since most information comes to the media from sources. Reporters can use their observations and opinions at times, but they usually do not personally witness news events. They must rely on second-hand observations.

Direct Quotes

Direct quotes lend authenticity and credibility to news stories. By reproducing the exact words, a writer is putting the reader or listener in touch with the source. This adds color, interest and vitality to the news report. A story of any length needs direct quotes sprinkled through it to make it come alive.

Routine background or commonplace facts should not be used as direct quotation. The writer must be selective about what is used inside the quote marks and that should not include lifeless and verbose material that could be summarized. The reader and listener expect direct quotes to offer controversy, emotion, color, interest, individual perspective and impact.

Direct quotes cannot be changed, except for the correction of minor mistakes, since spoken language is not as formal as written. Direct quotes should be brief, one or two sentences. They should usually be in separate paragraphs so they stand out from the rest of the story.

Direct quotes properly placed can greatly help the transition and readability of a story. They should be alternated with paragraphs of summary and paraphrase. Some editors like a rough ratio of two paragraphs of summary or paraphrase to one paragraph of direct quote.

The best quotes flow naturally out of the paragraphs immediately above them in the story by amplifying, elaborating and explaining the summary that has gone before. Look at the way direct quotation is used in the first paragraphs of this Associated Press story:

> HOUSTON (AP)—Harry Kamion cheated death more than once as a captain in the Polish underground during World War II, surviving torture by Gestapo officers.

The odds caught up with the 67-year-old businessman when he was gunned down during a robbery.

"The war couldn't do it, the Nazis couldn't do it. But here in Houston—far, far away from the terrible past—a simple hoodlum took his life," said Kamion's wife, Evelyn.

Kamion was shot three times in the chest and once in the wrist Saturday morning at his plumbing store, detectives said.

A store employee said Kamion begged the robber, "Don't shoot me," but the gunman ignored the plea. Kamion died as an ambulance sped to Ben Taub Hospital.

Detectives said Sunday they had no suspects and were uncertain how much money or property the robber took.

"Its the same old thing," said homicide detective J.H. Benford. "The man had been at that location for 22 years. Everybody liked him; he gave people credit when they needed it." **(Used by permission of The Associated Press.)**

Notice how the third paragraph follows naturally after the first two paragraphs. The quote adds impact and perspective. The other direct quotes—in the fifth and seventh paragraphs—are logically related to material in the preceding paragraphs. The quotes help paint a graphic picture for the reader.

Indirect quotation is used in the fourth and sixth paragraphs. Those paragraphs are summaries or paraphrases of what detectives said. Notice that attribution or speech tags are present to identify the speakers.

Partial quotation can be used effectively in news stories for a few words or a phrase spoken or written by a source. Here's an example:

Mayor John White said his opponent "could not be trusted" with the office. (Partial quote)

This technique can be overdone and should be used sparingly.

When one source is quoted immediately after another in a news story, a new paragraph should be used. Many times a paragraph of paraphrase in between will aid the transition.

Direct quotes have to be punctuated properly or the reader will be confused. Remember that with a continual direct quotation of more than one paragraph in length, closing quote marks are omitted at the end of each paragraph except the last one.

Most editors frown on direct quote leads, but partial quote leads sometimes can be used. The direct quote lead can become a crutch for the beginning writer who has difficulty summarizing a story. Most direct quotes do not summarize a straight news story, but they might be used in rare instances on feature stories or personality profiles.

Indirect Quotes

An indirect quote, as mentioned earlier, is a paraphrase or summary of what a source said or wrote. Quote marks are not used, but the attribution should be made clear. The speaker's words are rephrased by the writer, but the substance of what the speaker said should be maintained. It is unprofessional and unethical to change the meaning of what a source said or wrote.

Details, background and essential facts can be included concisely with indirect quotes because the writer can summarize what might be rambling statements by a source. The indirect quote is used basically to present information in a story.

Verbs of Attribution

Verbs of attribution are used to assign words and sentences to the source who originated them. The English language has hundreds of such verbs, but many of them are troublesome because they are loaded with connotative meaning.

The best verb of attribution in most instances is "said" because it is neutral and means to speak words. Print journalists usually use the past tense while broadcasters favor the present tense "say" because it connotes immediacy.

Other verbs can be used for attribution, but only when they accurately reflect the exact meaning of the words. Writers must be aware of these differences. For example, "stated" is not a good synonym for said because it has a formal connotation. "Assert" means to express a strongly held view or opinion and "declare" should be reserved for declarations.

Such verbs as "revealed" and "disclosed" imply the unveiling of unknown or secret information. They should be used only in correct circumstances. "Admitted" is a loaded word that should be used only when someone is actually admitting something. "Denied" is equally suspect because it implies guilt on the part of the speaker.

"Pointed out" and "noted" can be used when the speaker is

expressing a statement of fact. Said is often better. "According to" should be used with inanimate sources such as "according to the statute" or "according to the textbook." "Explain" means to explain or make something understandable. It is not a good synonym for said. "Add" implies that the quote is of less importance than what has gone before. "Comments" has a similar meaning.

"Claim" is not a proper synonyn for said because it tends to cast doubt on the veracity of the speaker. Also, claim is more properly used when persons are claiming something that rightfully belongs to them, such as their hats. "Announced" should be used only with the first formal statement about something. "Charged" implies serious criticism, almost like criminal or moral wrongdoing.

Verbs of attribution do not include such non-verbal expressions as "grinned," "smiled" or "laughed." Words cannot be grinned, smiled or laughed. Words, however, can be said with a grin or said with a smile or a laugh.

There are many verbs of attribution. Most have connotative meanings beyond the simple fact of speaking words and should be used only in their proper context. The writer must not be afraid to use "said" repeatedly for attribution.

Where to Place Attribution

Direct Quotes

The most common place for attribution in a direct quotation is at the end of the first sentence, or the first natural break in a long sentence. Attribution at the end or in the middle of a direct quote is preferred because this places the emphasis on the quotation itself, yet quickly identifies the source:

"One prisoner escaped," the sheriff said. "We stopped the others before they had a chance to get away."

Placing the attribution at the end of a long sentence, or at the end of several sentences, would delay identification of the speaker. Rarely should the source begin a direct quotation:

The sheriff said, "One prisoner escaped. We stopped the others before they had a chance to get away."

The example above places too much emphasis on the source and weakens the impact of the direct quote. This structure should be used only when shifting to a new source after quoting someone else in the paragraph immediately above. If the source isn't identified at the beginning of the new direct quote, the reader will not know the speaker has changed. Note that only one attribution is needed for a continuous direct quotation:

"The shots came from the building across the street," Smith said.
"Whoever it was managed to get away in the confusion.
"The police have a description and we expect an arrest will be made soon."

Only one attribution is needed for the three paragraphs. This would be true no matter how many paragraphs as long as they were continuous. Also notice that the closing quote marks are used only at the end of the final paragraph.

Indirect Quotes

The writer should remember that every sentence of indirect quotation requires attribution. This is unlike direct quotes which need only one attribution if continuous. The quote marks tell the reader that the statement is attributed. Without attribution, a sentence of indirect quotation will be attributed to the reporter:

Williams said the council should take immediate action on the proposal. He said maintaining an adequate water supply was vital for the city.

In the preceding example, the second sentence requires attribution even though it is in the same paragraph with a sentence that has attribution. Unless all sentences of an indirect quote are attributed, the reader will not clearly understand who is making the statement. Attribution for indirect quotes can be placed at the beginning, in the middle or at the end of each statement. Location will depend on which element is being emphasized. Also, the location can be varied to prevent monotony:

Smith said the senators should have all the facts before making a decision. (Beginning)
The senators should have all the facts before making a decision, Smith said. (At the end of statement)
The man entered the hotel about noon, Smith

said, and asked to speak with the diplomat from Lebanon.
(In the middle of long sentence)

Speeches

Meetings, conventions, news conferences and speeches are among the most common events covered by reporters. These events are similar in that they involve the spoken word. The media writer's main objective is to write a clear and complete story, accurately conveying to the reader/listener/viewer the gist of what was said.

Speech stories are often the first assignments given to beginning reporters. It is important to learn the basics of speech story writing because the techniques can be applied to many other kinds of stories. The news writer covering a speech must use the methods of direct and indirect quotation mentioned earlier in this chapter. A writer frequently will need to do research about the speaker and the topic. Research will familiarize the reporter with the subject. Research techniques are discussed in chapter 7.

Being familiar with the topic will aid the writer to recognize new and important points the speaker might make. Experienced reporters develop the ability to listen and take notes at the same time. Some complete sentences are needed for direct quotes, but most notes consist of key words and phrases that capture the theme and major points in the speech. A reporter should not try to take down verbatim everything a speaker says.

The lead of a speech story often begins with a paraphrase of the major point or points made by the speaker. The attribution or speech tag is included and fastened grammatically to the indirect quote. The lead can begin with the speaker's name and identification when the name is well known, as is often the case. Frequently, however, what was said is more newsworthy and should go first:

> Summer job prospects for teen-agers in this area are dismal, Mayor William Milford said Thursday.
> "The unemployment rate is high, and we can expect it to go even higher for young people," he said.
> Milford spoke to approximately 150 business and civic leaders at a monthly meeting of the Chamber of Commerce.

The second paragraph is a direct quotation which supports the lead, and the occasion of the speech is dropped to the third paragraph. Beginning reporters often make a common mistake by writing what is known as a "say nothing" lead on speech stories:

> Mayor William Milford spoke Thursday to the Chamber of Commerce about the prospects of summer employment for teen-agers in this area.

The example above tells the reader nothing specifically about what the mayor said. Writing that he "spoke about" teen-age unemployment is vague. The lead places too much emphasis on the occasion and neglects the newsworthy aspect of the speech. Editors—and readers—quickly reject such leads.

Some speakers will cover several "themes" or major points and the writer might have to choose one or two for the lead. A lead that tries to cover four or five or more points will become crowded. One way to keep a lead from becoming cluttered is to use an indefinite identification of the speaker in the first paragraph and move the proper name lower:

> Acid rain is killing fish and destroying plant life in some lakes of eastern Canada, a leading scientist said Thursday.
>
> Dr. Thomas Wilson said testing stations around the lakes have confirmed the presence of acid pollution in rain and ground water.

Such background information as audience reaction or more identification of the speaker can be woven into the story in lower paragraphs. The body of a speech story consists mainly of alternating direct and indirect quotations plus background inserted by the writer. As mentioned earlier, most of the story should be paraphrased material. Direct quotations should be limited to no more than one-third of the story. This guideline is not ironclad and can be broken when direct quotes are colorful, important and necessary for the story.

Pre-Speech Story

A story is often written in advance of a speech to inform the public about the appearance of a speaker. Length and detail of this story will depend on the newsworthiness of the speaker and the topic to be discussed. The exact time and place are important elements for this story. Adequate identification of the speaker and the occasion are also necessary. The pre-speech is usually shorter than the speech story. Here's an example:

Mayor John Lofton will speak on goals for the city at a meeting of the Chamber of Commerce at 8 p.m. Thursday in the Pioneer Room of the Brown Hotel.

The pre-speech story can have other angles for the lead such as the topic or the occasion. These should be used only when they are most newsworthy.

Speech Story Example

Examine the following typical speech story from the **Fort Worth Star-Telegram.** Notice how direct and indirect quotations are used, how attribution is placed, which verbs of attribution are used and how background is inserted.

AUSTIN—Gov. Mark White told a group of high school principals today that he will call a special legislative session to deal with increased funding for education.

The governor, speaking to the Texas Association of Secondary Principals, said he will summon lawmakers back to Austin as soon as a special study committee on education completes its work.

"I don't intend to wait two full years before we address in the Legislature the problems of education," White said. "We must not delay. We cannot delay further the addressing of the issue of education."

White's remarks to the principals were his most definite comments to date on his plans for the Legislature. Lawmakers are not scheduled to reconvene in regular session until January 1985.

White assured the principals that the study committee, which was created at the insistance of House Speaker Gib Lewis, is not a stall tactic. He said he expects the panel to complete its work quickly, but did not give any specific deadline.

"This is not an excuse for further delay," he said. "Most of what we need to know has already been studied.

White said one of the primary tasks of the study committee is re-examining and compiling previous reports on the state's education needs.

Lewis, who opposed White's call for a tax increase during the regular session, has said he will support a tax hike if the study concludes it is needed to finance quality education.

White told the school principals he was "disappointed" that legislators did not increase teacher salaries during the regular session but insisted he will not give up.

"Sam Houston didn't win but one battle—the last one. The battle I intend to win is the last one on education," he said.

Leaders of the principals' group, which is holding a summer workshop at the Austin Hilton, pledged to help White push for a tax hike. The principals gave White a standing ovation when he entered and left the meeting and interrupted his speech several times with applause. **Used by permission, Fort Worth Star-Telegram.**

Exercises--Chapter 4

I. Write a pre-speech story based on the following facts:

At 8 p.m. next Thursday night; a Houston real estate developer by name of John Briggs at Holiday Inn; at monthly meeting of Business Boosters Club; will speak on Real Estate Trends During the 1980s.

II. Write a pre-speech story based on the following facts:

The Reverend Earl Callaway; at conference of Gospel Church members; in American Hotel; he will speak at 8 p.m. Monday; he is pastor of First Gospel Church; he is former missionary to Burma. He will talk on Increase in Christianity in Burma.

III. You are assigned to cover a speech by Millard Reynolds, Ph.D., a psychologist from New York City. He spoke at 8 p.m. last night in the Hilton Hotel to the Parent-Teacher Association. About 200 persons were in attendance. Below is a copy of his remarks.

Good evening ladies and gentlemen. I am delighted to talk to you about a recent development in our society--the growth of video games.

A whole array of problems including truancy, vandalism, drug and alcohol use, poor posture and even eye strain have been blamed on video games, especially on video arcades.

I am here to tell you not to worry. Video games are not that bad.

Recent research reveals youngsters are not becoming addicted to the games. For example, it is estimated that 80 percent of boys between ages of 14 and 18 spend less than $5 a week on the games.

Skeptical parents can relax. Experts find that the video arcade is to the younger generation what the corner ice cream store or drive-in restaurant was to their parents. It is mainly a pastime to reduce boredom.

Ninety-five percent of youngsters in a recent study in California of 1,000 teen-agers say no drug sales take place in arcades. The young people say drugs decrease the skillfulness of play and are discouraged by video playing. The youngsters say they spend half of their time in an arcade playing and the rest of the time watching others play.

Research indicates that a lot of socializing goes on in the arcades. I believe this is a major benefit from the video games. Some teen-agers who might be withdrawn or shunned by others make friends because the arcade environment encourages social interaction. I view it as perfectly normal behavior on the part of young people who are looking for a little excitement.

IV. Write a story based on the remarks made at 10 a.m. today by Police Chief Fred Byrd. He held a press conference in City Hall. The following are direct quotations:

"Crime—especially burglary—increases in the city during the summer. This summer we are planning to try several things to reduce the crime rate. Burglars stole $1.1 million in property from citizens here last summer.

"The city police will step up patrols in high-crime neighborhoods. We plan to use patrolmen on foot, on bicycle and mounted on horses. We are also training postal, newspaper and public utility workers to spot potential burglars.

"We are concentrating on crime prevention. This is probably the most ambitious program the police department has ever undertaken.

"We want citizen involvement also. A reward of $200 will be paid to citizens for information that leads to a conviction of a residential burglar."

V. Rewrite the following passive voice sentences into active voice.

1. A 2 percent pay increase was proposed by the governor.
2. The fire was fought by firefighters from three cities.
3. The speech was given by Sen. David White.
4. The ball was struck by the batter.
5. The house was damaged by high winds.

VI. Rewrite the following sentences to eliminate wordiness, redundancies, and/or misplaced modifiers.

1. The balloon landed in the vicinity of the church.
2. The game was called off due to the fact that it rained.
3. Shooting his best round, the golf ball dropped into the cup.
4. An autopsy on the body revealed the man had been strangled to death.
5. The group disclosed for the first time the future plans for the building.
6. The man decided to postpone his trip until later.
7. The student commuted back and forth to school.
8. The auditorium was filled to capacity for the program on Easter Sunday.
9. He said that at the present time the insurance business was an excellent one.
10. The two groups were combined together.
11. The business suffered losses estimated to be about the sum of $100,000.
12. At the conclusion of the conference, the council reached an agreement on the plan.
13. The actual facts are that for a period of several weeks she lived here.
14. The car came to a stop at the corner of Elm and Pine streets.
15. A large number of students are currently enrolled in the school.
16. She welcomed her fellow classmates to the first annual reunion.
17. The new recruit was introduced for the first time to the group.
18. The trip will last for a period of 20 days.
19. They told the interested listeners that summer time was best for business.
20. He went in order to hear the speaker.

VII. Rewrite to correct any attribution problems that might be present in the following sentences or paragraphs.

    1. "The plane was late" he said "and we were eager to get home."

    2. Smith said he was glad to win. "I feel like I was lucky. I had a strong opponent."

    3. "Math is my best subject," she said. "But I also like English."

    4. "There is the end of the trail," he grinned.

    5. "William lost the ball." "I was there when it happened," Scott expostulated.

    6. Gordon said the crop was ruined because of neglect. The boys failed to take proper care of it.

    7. "I heard Carter say, "Don't use that door," when the guest left," Johnson told the police.

    8. "It looks like a nice day," he asserted.

    9. "Reagan is our greatest president," he pointed out.

    10. "The committee just couldn't decide what to do, and the delegates were beginning to get disgusted. I don't really blame them for what they did," he said.

    VIII. Rewrite the following direct quotes into indirect quotes.

    1. "We're looking at alternatives to all the issues," Smith said.

    2. "There's going to be a lot of traffic in the area," he said, "but we're going to go ahead with the plan."

    3. "The Dallas ordinance is not as comprehensive as the San Diego ordinance," he said.

    4. Williams said, "The defendant has organized an illegal scheme to evade taxes."

    5. "Oil is a big gamble. It's a high-stakes game with millions bet on the outcome," he said.

5

Broadcast Style

Broadcast news writing is closely related to writing for print. A journalist who has mastered the basic techniques of newspaper style should have little trouble adapting to broadcast writing. Broadcast and print should not be thought of as separate kinds of journalism. Accuracy, fairness and objectivity apply to both. Both are aimed at a mass audience and follow the ethics and responsibilities of the news profession. The differences are in the manner of delivery. In a nutshell, broadcast news is largely for the ear–to be heard instead of to be read.

Broadcasters know that listeners don't get a second chance–they can't go back and reread the story. Listeners must grasp the story the first time they hear it, so the broadcast language must be clear, simple and conversational. Also the broadcast story is often limited to one minute or less of air time. This means the story might have to be told in fewer than 100 words, and many of the details in a newspaper story eliminated. The average news announcer reads about 150 words a minute.

A newspaper story of 20 to 30 or more paragraphs might be reduced to two or three sentences in a typical news broadcast. A good rule for the beginning broadcast writer is: write it the way you talk. An informal conversational style is easiest to understand. The present tense is used when possible, and the writing follows the way a person ordinarily speaks. Sentences are short and simple, even shorter than newspaper sentences. Active voice verbs are preferred. Notice how the following newspaper lead would be rewritten for broadcast:

The City Council voted today to increase the monthly garbage collection fee from $5 to $10 a household effective next month. (Newspaper.)

The monthly fee for garbage collection is going up next month. The City Council has increased it to ten dollars a household. (Broadcast.)

The lead paragraph of the broadcast example above is broken into two sentences, changed to present tense and the word today is eliminated. Experienced broadcast news writers often write as though they were talking to a friend or neighbor. Some of the formality of printed journalism can be forgotten. The goal is to make it sound more like normal conversation, yet keep it concise.

Contractions are conversational and acceptable for broadcast, but slang, colloquial, off-color and flagrantly nongrammatical expressions are not. Sentence fragments are acceptable, and it is all right to repeat. The fleeting nature of broadcast means that listeners need to be reminded of major points and key names:

> Three persons were arrested today and charged with operating a drug ring in the city, Pottsville police said. (Newspaper.)
> A drug bust in Pottsville. . . Pottsville police have arrested three persons on drug trafficking charges. Police say the arrests have cracked a major drug ring in the city. (Broadcast.)

The broadcast version above repeats the words drug, police, arrest and Pottsville. Repeating proper nouns rather than using a pronoun can help the listener. Here's another broadcast example:

> The governor...James Green...says the highway bill needs changing. Green says more money is required for bridge repairs.

Identification is usually first in the sentence to alert the listener of who the source is. This technique, which differs from that used in most newspaper sentences, helps grab the listener's attention before the important details are revealed. Such cues tell the listener to perk up, pay attention because key information is coming:

> A source close to Governor Harold Wilson says the governor plans to run again.
> Assistant street superintendent Marty Cohen says the highway will open in ten days.

The key facts are often delayed until the end of a broadcast sentence as in the examples above.

Attribution is as important for broadcast as for print, but the placement differs. The source precedes the message in the sentence. The listener needs to be cued when direct quotations are going to be used in a broadcast. There are no quote marks to indicate a source's exact words. Saying "quote-unquote" before and after every direct quote is one way, but that method is shunned by most broadcasters because it is jarring to the ear and interrupts the flow of the sentence. Broadcasters favor inserting phrases into the sentence to tip the listener to expect a direct quote:

> The councilman says...in these words..."The council is not in favor of this plan."
> The senator says...and these are his words..."Taxes will have to be raised."
> The mayor rejects what he calls "a flagrant power play on the part of the developers."
> Senator Wilson says...as he puts it..."The committee must be taught a lesson."

Broadcast style differs from print on use of punctuation marks. More dashes and ellipses are used to add emphasis...and to allow the news announcer to take a breath. Hyphens are used between letters in abbreviations such as F-B-I or C-I-A.

Broadcasters usually spell out numbers to help announcers: The F-B-I says thirty-nine arrests were made in the raids. Symbols such as the dollar sign should not be used in broadcast style. They should be spelled out like this: Twenty-dollars instead of $20.

The listener needs to be told where a story takes place. There are no printed datelines, and phrases such as "here today" are confusing in broadcast copy. A broadcast signal might cover a wide area and many listeners won't know from which city it originates. The where often needs to be included. The wire services include a datelines, but the where is written into the copy also:

> (Smithville)—The Smithville school board has a problem...The board can't agree on what to name a new elementary school.

Remember, broadcast copy is written to be read by a news announcer. The writer should reread a story aloud, or at least under his breath, to hear how it sounds. Long complex sentences that leave an announcer gasping for air are to be avoided.

Exercises: Chapter 5

I. Write the following indirect quotes into broadcast style.

1. Tests on the insecticide will take two years, a spokesman for the Agriculture Department said.
2. The settlement of the suit, Councilman Jack Dalton said, meant the city would collect about $100,000.
3. The bank was not able to find the records, Jay Brown, bank vice president, said today.
4. County Commissioner T.L. Sanders, who spent two hours before a grand jury today, said he was sure he would not be indicted.

II. Rewrite the following direct quotes into direct quotes for broadcast.

1. "All 10 victims died within minutes," Fire Chief Sam Baker said.
2. "The plan should definitely be rejected," Mayor Charles Brandt said.
3. "I never knew my real name," Mrs. Callahan said. "Now I know, and I couldn't be happier.
4. "The festival was a celebration of love," rock singer Sara Perkins said.

III. Rewrite the following UPI newspaper stories into broadcast style stories of about 150 words each. **(Stories used by permission of UPI.)**

United Press International

MOSCOW—The Soviet cruise ship that crashed into a railroad bridge Sunday on the Volga River toppled a freight train on the vessel, killing as many as 400 people, an area resident said Wednesday.

"There is great chaos in the city. People are crying in the streets," the resident of Ulyanovak said in a telephone call to a relative in Moscow, 450 miles west.

The caller, whose account could not be independently verified, said only 40 survivors were found from the wreck of the diesel-powered Alexander Suvorov.

The vessel could carry 466 passengers and a large crew.

The report of 400 deaths would make it the worst Soviet disaster in recent years, surpassing last year's air crash that killed 90 people, and a train wreck in 1981 in which 70 passenger died.

A spokesman for the Soviet travel agency Intourist said Tuesday there were at least 100 deaths.

According to the resident's account, a freight train toppled onto the cruise boat when the four-deck vessel struck the railroad bridge.

The impact tore off the crowded top deck where passengers were watching a movie.

The ship's command may have failed to negotiate the opening in the bridge or incorrectly gauged the river level, the Intourist official said.

There were no accounts of the disaster in the Soviet press beyond an announcement from the government and the Communist party expressing sympathy for the families of the dead. It gave no death toll.

The official statement was unusual, since Soviet authorities generally keep such matters quiet unless foreigners are involved. There were no foreigners in this case, the Intourist spokesman said.

Another indication of the scope of the tragedy was the appointment of a panel headed by a full Politburo member, First Deputy Premier Geydar Aliyev, to investigate.

The panel included officials of the Railways Ministry, adding weight to reports that a train was involved.

The Czech-built Suvorov was named after an 18th-century field marshal who led Russian forces in warfare against France.

United Press International

COLOGNE, West Germany—Rain-swollen rivers forced hundreds of people to flee Sunday as torrents of water flooded the Rhine wine-growing regions of West

Germany.

Army troops ferried supplies to stranded villages along the Rhine and Mosel rivers, which officials said rose 28 feet above normal in the worst flooding in 38 years.

In Cologne, the Rhine burst its banks for the second time in six weeks and flooded the medieval city center. Flooding also was reported in Coblenz, Bernkastel-Kues and Trier. In Remagen, authorities ordered residents to boil drinking water to reduce the chances of illness from contamination.

Flooding also hit Bonn, and fire crews fought to save the Parliament building from water damage. Police said fire pumps were working continually to remove water from the building.

Vintners said rain and floods had caused extensive damage to vines and threatened to wreck the autumn grape harvest.

Rainfall for May was the highest recorded for more than a century.

United Press International

HOUSTON—A stuntman who climbed a Houston skyscraper in March was acquitted Wednesday of trespassing.

Charges against Ron Broyles, 29, of Los Angeles, were dismissed by a judge who said the evidence against Broyles was not sufficient to convict him.

Broyles, who wore a white tuxedo and ruffled shirt for the climb, scaled the granite and glass exterior of the 75-story Texas Commerce Tower on March 14. He was arrested at the top of the building by police who booked him in the city jail.

But Harris County Court-at-Law Judge Alfred Leal dismissed the three-woman, three-man jury and dropped charges against Broyles, saying the state could not convict the climber based on the evidence presented during the first and only day of the trial.

"We can all admire Mr. Broyles and his

accomplishment, but at the same time we can all shiver a little at his feat and the danger that goes along with it," Leal told the jury. "The circumstances of this case are unique. I don't think it will set a precedent."

Defense attorney Jim Moriarty argued that Broyles did not violate the trespassing law because he left the building as soon as possible.

Moriarty said he believed the charges were dismissed because of "the testimony by the building manager who said there were only two safe ways off the building—up or down—and the option was left up to Mr. Broyles. He went up.

"He was told to get off and he did," Moriarty said.

Trespassing charges still are pending against another man who scaled Houston's 71-story Allied Bank Plaza last month. David Hancock Jr., who identified himself as the "Blue Bandit," also faces charges of evading arrest.

Broyles appeared dazed Wednesday. "I'm still kind of interested to find out how this will affect other cases. I kind of feel responsible for the Blue Bandit."

But he proudly wore a black T-shirt which stated "Official Member Thousand Foot Club," an organization of climbers who have scaled skyscrapers over 1,000 feet.

United Press International

DETROIT—Children who are under emotional or physical stress have lower scores on intelligence tests than healthier youngsters, researchers said Sunday.

Bernard Brown and Lilian Rosenbaum of Georgetown University created a stress index using a sample of 4,000 7-year-old children.

"What we found was that the stress index showed the IQ of the children decreased 13 percent from low stress to high stress," Brown said in an interview after addressing the annual meeting of the American Association for the Advancement of Science.

The youngsters' IQ scores averaged 104 with no

stress and 91 with high stress, he said.

The researchers did not test children before and after they were under stress but compared children who were under stress with those who were not.

"IQs decreased much more for children who were held back a grade or assigned to special education, and there was a particularly dramatic change for children who had eye problems, the ones who had less than 20-60 vision.

The stress factors included poor vision, hearing, muscle tone or reflex problems, behavioral trouble such as crying, nail-biting and hyperactivity, and assignment to a special education class.

"But we also looked at the parents in the family–the health of the family," Ms. Rosenbaum said.

Examples were the number of times the family moved, death in the family, divorce, the number of children in the family and the parents' employment status and income.

"A child or adult who is functioning at normal, to bright might be that much brighter–10 percent more intelligent–were that person not under X number of stresses," Ms. Rosenbaum said.

So far, the research "suggests that stress is a cumulative thing," she said. For instance, a child might have moved six times in four years, have poor vision and perhaps (have experienced) a death in the family.

"We knew before that stress affected the body and affected physical and emotional behavior. We are now saying it also affects intellectual functioning," Brown said.

United Press International

OTTAWA–A former Royal Canadian Mounted Police officer involved in counter-intelligence was arrested on charges that he passed secret information to Soviet agents more than 25 years ago, the police force said Wednesday.

The police said that James Douglas Finley Morrison–who had once used the code name "Long Knife" in his espionage work—was arrested Tuesday in Prince Rupert, British Columbia.

He was to appear before a justice of the peace in Ottawa Thursday for a bail hearing, an aide to Attorney General Mark MacGuigan said.

According to an order MacGuigan signed June 1, Morrison, 67, spied for the Soviets between April 1, 1955 and Jan. 31, 1958.

Although the government knew about the case since 1977, an aide said "sufficient evidence to warrant institution of proceedings first came to the attention of the minister within the last month."

The charges alleged Morrison "unlawfully communicated to another person, or persons, including Nicolai Ostrovsky and Rem Krassilnikov, agents of a foreign power, namely the Union of Soviet Socialist Republics, secret information."

Krassilnikov at the time was the third secretary in the Soviet Embassy. Ostrovsky was named in John Sawatsky's book "For Services Rendered" as a Soviet spy. Sawatsky, a former journalist, is the author of several books on Canadian intelligence.

Morrison, who was recruited in the security service in 1950 and left in 1958, is also charged with passing secrets he had obtained while a member of the RCMP and with conspiring with Ostrovsky and Krassilnikov to collect state secrets.

The "Long Knife" case came to public attention last year after publication of "For Services Rendered."

Solicitor General Robert Kaplan said in the House of Commons the government was first informed of the case in 1977 by the RCMP. "At that time," he said, "they were advised there was insufficient evidence to mount a prosecution either under the Official Secrets Act or under the Criminal Code."

Sawatsky's book said "Long Knife" had worked in counter-intelligence assigned to watch activities of Soviet personnel in Canada. He was involved in the case of a Soviet spy, code-named Gideon, who was recruited by Canadian intelligence to act as a double agent.

Gideon returned to Moscow and was believed to

have been executed.

Morrison was transferred from Ottawa to Winnipeg, where he was living when he left the force.

At the time of his arrest, Morrison was working as a safety coordinator.

6

Interviewing for the Media

In this age of communications revolutions, man is bombarded with information. He receives so many messages that he figuratively "swims" in a sea of communication flotsam and jetsam. He is dependent upon the media for facts about the world. That information is as accurate as the reporter is careful and precise in making observations, seeking out sources and analyzing and sorting data. Reporters become the eyes and ears for mass man. As such, they must understand the principal methods of gathering information.

Media reporters use three basic techniques to get material for news and feature stories. They are (1) direct observation, (2) secondary sources and (3) interviewing. The most often used information-gathering tool is the interview because it is quick and economical. Let us look at each information-gathering method briefly and then move into a more complete discussion of interviewing.

Direct Observation

Direct observation becomes part of virtually every news and feature story. Reporters who cover a city council meeting, a school board meeting, a criminal trial, etc., use direct observation to glean information necessary to build the story. But they usually combine it with interviewing by calling sources to verify or to elaborate.

Observation is a neat, convenient way to research a topic, and it is liked by reporter and reader/viewer/listener. Direct observation, on the surface, appears the most accurate, most reliable method of information gathering. It involves eyewitness accounts, a "you are there" concept. What could be more accurate than an eyewitness account? There are a number of serious flaws to this method of information gathering, however. First, individuals see an event from different perspectives. The message imprinted on one's mind is influenced by his background. That is, one's frame of reference becomes a part of the event. A truer "picture" often is a composite drawn from observations of sources who view an event from different angles. Observing, and then interviewing as many sources as necessary, is a better approach.

Second, perspective can depend on where an individual stands in relation to the event. The different angles from which one views something determine to some extent what is "seen." Look at it from a viewer's perspective on a rainbow: where is the end of the rainbow? That depends on where one is standing at the time.

And, third, it's physically impossible for reporters to be at all events. Editors are not psychic. They can't foresee events and dispatch reporters to them.

Secondary Sources

Reporters obtain and verify information from secondary sources. Here we refer to information contained in news clips (commonly called the morgue), basic reference books, public records and opinion polls. The morgue provides the reporter background on a news event, the reference books and public records provide verification of facts and figures, and the polls provide background materials as well as information for analyzing statements made by sources. They are beginning points in the information-gathering process. These sources are covered in Chapter 7.

Interviewing

The methods listed above are part of the reporting process. But, the backbone of information gathering is the interview. It has been defined variously. John Gunther called it a purposeful conversation which implies that a reporter goes into the task with a purpose. The reporter does not have a preconceived notion of what the story will be. Instead he approaches an interview with an open mind and with a knowledge base that helps him to ask questions that will guide the source.

Journalism and mass communication use the word unterviewing in at least four ways. The definitions determine format and content of the story which the reporter writes. The four approaches are (1) interview for facts, (2) interview story, (3) interview profile, and (4) talk-show interview. A brief discussion of each will further define the concept.

Interview For Facts

In the interview for facts, the reporter uses interview traditionally. For example, a reporter is assigned to cover a meeting of the board of regents. He goes to the meeting, sits through the deliberations, takes notes and gathers the facts for a news story or stories. Let's say that the regents pass a resolution to ban automobiles from campus beginning with the fall semester.

The reporter talks with the regent who introduced the resolution, with regents who voted in favor, with regents who voted against and with the university president. The reporter is interviewing for facts to flesh out the story. Further, the reporter talks with (interviews) students at random to gain another perspective. Again, he interviews for facts.

Interview Story

The reporter covering the regents meeting tells the editor there's going to be adverse reaction to the regents' resolution to ban cars from campus. A student, Kevin Smythe, called last night to tell the reporter that a group had organized to oppose the ban. The reporter interviews Smythe about the group's plans. The story is an interview story. It is a new development on a story that delves more deeply into a situation.

Interview Profile

While at Smythe's apartment for the interview, the reporter notices a large collection of matchbooks. Matchbooks line the walls of the living room. The reporter makes note of the collection. He decides to do a feature story about Smythe's hobby. Here the reporter is using the third meaning of interview: a profile interview for a feature story. In this type, the reporter primarily is a listener. One of the main purposes of the profile interview is to get the "flavor" of the individual and to develop information around which to build a story in the fashion of the story-teller.

Talk-Show Interview

The fourth meaning is derived from on the air talk shows such as Donahue, Meet the Press, etc. One function of the interviewer is to listen. He opens up the principal with a few choice questions and gently guides the speaker. The host's role is one of encouraging the person to talk about the subject of interest to the viewer/listener.

Now, let's return to the general topic of interviewing and more specifics about the process. Interviewing is a basic tool of the journalism profession; an estimated 80 percent of the content of the news media comes from interviews. It is used in virtually every news situation. The reporter is the conduit through which flows social, political and economic information. It is a process which demands hard work, and it can be divided into two stages: (1) Pre-Interview Research and (2) The Interview.

Pre-Interview Research

If the interview is viewed as a purposeful conversation, it follows logically that reporters must know what they want to know. That's another way of saying reporters must research their topics before interviews. A successful interview is about 90 percent preparation and 10 percent interviewing. In preparing, reporters may find a three-step process helpful. The steps are (1) researching the topic and the person or persons to be interviewed, (2) devising a tentative theme for the story and (3) preparing tentative questions.

Research is essential if the reporter is to be able to ask the right questions and to understand the answers. Pre-interview research makes the reporter more credible to the source and the source feels more at ease in sharing information. Prepared reporters communicate that the interview is a serious matter and that they have made an effort to understand the subject.

With preparation, reporters are better able to ask questions that add depth and understanding. The writer who interviews a university president about a tuition increase should find out how much the increase is, when the last increase was made and how the university compares with other universities on tuition costs.

Not only do preparations signal that reporters are serious, they save time. Sources are busy people. It is, therefore, important that an interviewer devise strategies to elicit information as quickly as possible. Research gives reporters background details and leaves the interview to discuss more significant issues.

News sources are not impressed with reporters who ask mundane questions such as "How do you spell your name?," or "Where did you begin your career in public administration?" But sources are impressed with reporters who ask questions such as "The proposed garbage disposal system is similar to the one at Peoria, Illinois, where you were assistant city manager. Do you foresee similar problems when the program is instituted here?" Such a question links the background of the source to the subject and opens the door for significant exchange of information. And the story provides information and understanding.

Preparation also enables reporters to be better watchdogs for society. This means they must be on the lookout for sources who try to manipulate them. An effective way to keep from being manipulated by news sources is to be well versed on a topic. Research puts reporters in a position to cope with misinformation attempts. Most news sources are honest with competent and ethical reporters. However, the newsgatherer must watch for the manipulator who tries to talk around a topic to avoid controversial subjects.

But there is another news source for whom pre-interview research is just as important. The shy, retiring source needs to be put at ease or opened up by the interviewer. Reporters who have knowledge of source and topic can use the information to help build trust between reporter and source.

Reporters who go into interviews with knowledge about sources' hobbies, interests, achievements, family members, etc., can more easily get the conversation moving. Once rapport has been established, the reporter can move into the topic. The writer can plan information-gathering strategies by knowing when to be tough, when to be kind or when to be sympathetic.

Many stories involve public officials in controversial situations. In such circumstances, the reporter uses pre-interview research as a guide to what to expect. For example, a writer is assigned to interview a minister for a follow-up on accusations that the World Council of Churches has channeled contributions to Communist causes. The minister may be incensed with the report. Some members of his congregation have threatened to cut off financial support unless the denomination withdraws from the World Council.

Here's where the reporter's background in research can come in handy. The reporter theorizes about the minister's attitude toward the subject and consequently toward the reporter. Based on the theorizing, the writer develops a plan of attack that meshes with the source's probable defenses. Research opens the door. It is the foundation upon which a strong news story will be built.

The reporter represents the public. His effectiveness is often directly related to research. It is a demanding task and tests a journalist. The plaintive cry: but how can a reporter working on a strict mass media deadline have the time to do so much research? The answer is clearcut: good reporters read widely and avidly. They soak up information like sponges. They constantly add to their knowledge base, and they become experts on issues and people in the town in which their newspaper or radio-tv station operates.

The Interview

Armed with information on the topic and the person to be interviewed, the reporter is ready to interview a source. Reporters should feel that they are quasi-experts. They approach the assignment as an educational experience. They use their information base to guide the conversation.

Also a reporter should approach every interview positively, agreeing that the source is honest and that the reporter intends to be ethical and responsible. An atmosphere of trust is essential or the news story can turn out to be reactions of the reporter and source to each other.

The reporter utilizes two broad types of interview questions: non-directed or open-ended, and directed or closed. Each has distinct roles in eliciting information, and conversely each has limitation and disadvantages. In any interview, however, the reporter will use both types to get a complete story.

Non-Directed Questions

The non-directed question is conversational and helps establish rapport with a source. It is designed to get a source to talk, to relax and to give serious thought to a topic. Such questions demand good listeners because they permit a source to talk openly and at length. Reporters using this type question can gain insight into a subject. This is a necessity for one writing feature stories or indepth articles about complex topics.

With a non-directed question, a reporter interviewing the superintendent of schools about a change in requirements for high school graduation might proceed as follows:

"Good morning, Superintendent. I am John Jones of the Daily Bugle, and we're doing a story about the new requirements for high school graduation. We've seen a number of reports on the need to upgrade course requirements. What is this all about? Tell me what these changes are going to accomplish."

The reporter has opened the door to a broad topic, and he must be ready to sit back and listen. The non-directed approach can encourage more depth from a source. The key to obtaining significant information is to tactfully engineer a source to cover points necessary for the assignment. Too, the non-directed question can create a warm and trusting atmosphere effective for getting truthful, serious responses. As with any news reporting tool, effectiveness improves as the experience of the reporter increases.

Disadvantages of the non-directed approach are time and control. The reporter on deadline does not have the luxury to spend hours with a source. When the reporter opens the door to a broad topic and invites the source to talk, he places the source in control. Under these conditions, the news source can steer the conversation and avoid critical and controversial topics.

Directed Questions

The most often used question is the directed or closed. The reporter is briefer; he controls the interview. Using the example with the superintendent of schools, the reporter might proceed as follows:

"Good morning, Superintendent. I am John Jones of the Daily Bugle, and we're doing a story about the new high school graduation requirements. Tell me, sir, what are the specific changes that will be made at your school?... Now, let's discuss that a little further: how will a foreign language better prepare the students for college and university study? ... Is it a proven fact that languages improve one's performance in English usage? . . . Now, tell me how the requirement of another year of science will upgrade the student's education?"

In this situation, the reporter gets to the point, asks direct and specific questions, follows up on evasive and incomplete answers with more specific questions.

While the directed question is generally effective, it can have negative effects on a source, resulting in misleading responses and thus misinformation. Since the reporter asks questions specifically and leaves little opportunity for the source to talk openly, the source may be influenced by the questions. If a source perceives that the reporter wants to hear only information related to the questions asked, he may not volunteer anything else.

For example, if a source thinks a reporter approves of a response, the source may repeat or overemphasize that idea. If the reporter's behavior conveys a disapproval to the source, he may discontinue discussion of that topic or simply "clam-up." One must keep in mind that everyone likes to have his ideas approved.

For some sources too many specific questions may discourage opening new and fruitful areas. In using closed or directed questions, the reporter must develop the ability to use probe questions. Probe questions direct the interviewee into areas where the reporter needs answers. The interviewer should use these questions when the interviewee strays from the topic, when a clearer answer is needed for something that has already been said, or when explanations, examples or comparisons are sought.

Useful probing questions may direct the source to rephrase his comments, to explain what he means or how he knows what he is saying is true. For example, the reporter interviewing the mayor about a garbage collection system asks a specific question about how the system will operate in Hometown. He gets a specific answer, and to illuminate the issue, he must use follow-up questions. He might say, for example, "Yes, Mayor Jones, I agree with your idea that we should explore ways to cut costs on garbage collection." The mayor loves the reporter because he agrees with him. To get the full impact of the question, however, it is necessary to probe. The reporter may follow with, "But Mayor Jones, you indicate that the garbage department has gone in the hole $150,000 for the past year. Do you believe that the new garbage collection program will result in substantial savings to the city?"

If he responds with "Yes...," the reporter will need to follow up with questions designed to obtain evidence. He may say, "Mayor Jones, can you give me examples where this type of system has been used and the results?"

Effectiveness of interviewing is dependent upon the style and phrasing of questions. The reporter needs to consider five problem areas in developing questions. **First, the questions must be objective.** That is, they must be designed to elicit information rather than reaction. Questions which evoke emotional responses do little to advance information. The questions must be clear, concise and neutral. Here's an example of a question that was asked by a student reporter: "President Rogers, don't you feel that the university's underhanded, more or less dishonest policy of using student parking fines to finance scholarships will tend to alienate student-administration relations?"

Look at this question: first, it is loaded with connotative words, or words that are emotion-evoking. "Underhanded," "dishonest policy," "alienate" appeal to the source's emotions and responses are likely to be reactions to the words. They may result in pithy and controversial statements but rarely in straight-forward and accurate information. The question should be re-worded. One revision might be, "President Rogers, do you feel that the university's policy of using parking fines to finance scholarships will affect the student-administration relations at the university? If so, how?"

Second, the questions should be answerable. That's another way of saying that the reporter should be specific. If the questions are ambiguous, broad as the proverbial side of the barn or highly philosophical, the reporter can expect to get the same type of answers. As an example, a reporter asks a local minister about the charges that the World Council of Churches funds are being diverted to aid Communists: "Reverend Smith, what is your opinion of the '60-Minutes' program on the World Council of Churches?" The question gives no beginning point, it gives no direction for the source to respond because it is so broad that it is unanswerable. Contrast the above question with this one: "Reverend Smith, a recent '60-Minutes' program reported that funds from the World Council of Churches were being channeled into projects labeled as Communist. Specifically, how are funds collected by the organization and assigned to projects?" This question gives a direction for the source; it provides a connection with the theme of the story. It is answerable.

The story is told that the late sports writer Grantland Rice spoke to a sophomore-level journalism class. One young student reporter asked, "Mr. Rice, what is your opinion of football?" The writer is reported to have responded, "I have many. . . what specifically did you want me to talk about?" Rice would have been correct to tell the reporter that the question was infantile and could elicit no plausible information. If a source is to answer a question adequately, the reporter must provide direction. A source takes cues from the interviewer; those cues should come from the reporter's overall theme.

Third, if one is to elicit accurate information about an event, he must word questions precisely right. News sources generally are not known for volunteering information. They accept that the reporter is in charge. The more controversial the news event, the greater the likelihood that a source will not volunteer information. If the reporter is in left field with a question, most sources will not lie to him, and they will not point him toward controversial information.

Let's say that reporter Joe is assigned to interview the mayor about a new location for the garbage landfill operation. The State Health Department has ordered the city to vacate the landfill within three months. Rumor is that the city is considering contracting the disposal operation to Out-of-Town Company. Joe meets with the mayor and asks, "Mayor Jones, I understand that the city is nearing a decision on relocation of the sanitary landfill. Can you tell me more specific details about the negotiations with the Out-of-Town Company?" The mayor says the city is working on the problem, but she knows nothing about the Out-of-Town Company negotiations.

Joe goes to other points, returns to the office and writes the story for the afternoon newspaper. On the local radio station's 5 o'clock news, the lead story announces that negotiations on the landfill relocation between the City and the State College administration are expected to be completed tomorrow. The story reports that the City and State College will operate it jointly. Editor Mack demands to know why Joe did not get the story. Joe returns to the mayor.

The mayor did not tell Joe about the City and State College negotiations because he did not ask about them. The reporter has learned the hard way that sources expect to be asked precise questions; ball-park questions do not elicit information. This example is hypothetical.

Here's an example from the real world. A few years ago news reports said that the CIA had attempted to raise a Soviet submarine in the North Atlantic. A reporter asked William Colby, then director of the CIA, about the sketchy story. Colby is reported to have said that the CIA had not attempted to raise a Russian sub in the Atlantic Ocean.

Later a news report quoted Colby that the CIA had tried to raise a Russian sub in the Pacific Ocean near Hawaii. To the reporter's complaint of misinformation, Colby said that he did not lie; the reporter did not ask about the Pacific Ocean.

Fourth, the reporter is advised to ask one question at a time. There are two primary reasons. First, when two questions are linked, one communicates the assumption that they are related. They may not be. Second, two joined questions require a source to do mental juggling. He must remember the questions while at the same time providing answers. Let's look at an example.

As a reporter Joe interviews the governor about a prison problem: "Governor, why do you think Judge Luther Banyon ruled as he did on the prison issue, and what do you think will be the political repercussions of the ruling?" That's two questions, and tied together they imply that the ruling is going to lead to political repercussions. That may or may not be true. Also, the source might answer only one part of the multiple question, the part he wants to answer and which may not be the most important.

The reporter's job is to ferret out information, present the ideas and let the reader/viewer/listener interpret. Another problem with the two questions above, of course, is that answering either is a mammoth undertaking and tying them together may result in overloading the source's information circuits. There is a need to break the question into units (separate questions) that give greater direction.

Finally, the reporter should not ask questions with repetitive clauses. Say something once and stop; don't repeat the question, even if phrased differently. Many well-meaning reporters insult their sources by providing too much interpretation. As an example, the reporter interviews a senator for a story on an impeachment charge. "Senator, could you explain by what process the Senate will consider the impeachment issue, and in what way this body of government will handle the case for removal of the president from office?" Ask the question only once. Tacking on the second version merely clouds the water.

Success in Interviewing

The reporter may ask all the right questions and come away with inadequate information. The art of interviewing demands that one develop the ability to listen and to relate to other people. Researchers have found that one block to good communication is a lack of listening skills. A good listener is marked by two distinct factors: silence and a genuine interest in others. A good listener asks a question and then concentrates on the answer. He is relaxed, confident and has no need to steer the conversation toward himself. He encourages communication by giving signals that say, "that's interesting. . . could you tell me more about that," or "I was not aware of that aspect of the situation. You certainly have excellent insight into your work; I'd like to hear more." This attitude communicates interest and concern. It creates an atmosphere of warmth that encourages exchange of ideas and opinions. One key to good interviewing is communicating to the source that the interviewer is doing more than a job. . . he is listening and learning. Silence, too, is a valuable tool to elicit comments. Sources generally do not like periods of silence.

A good listener is characterized by interest in people, patience in permitting a speaker to develop fully an idea and delayed reaction. The first of these characteristics is self-explanatory and has been covered above. The second merits a short explanation.

The reporter as a listener asks a question and permits the source to answer without interruption. The source may veer from the topic, but the good listener will permit him to finish his thoughts before interrupting to guide the discussion back on track. And no matter how much the reporter disagrees with the source, he will not argue. A listener also will not provide negative body language cues. A shake of the head, frown, switch in the chair, etc., tells the interviewee that the interviewer is displeased. These factors are subjective and should not become a part of the news-gathering process.

Developing listening skills is a constant process. To become proficient it is necessary, first of all, to develop an attitude of genuine interest in one's topic and to view people as unique, interesting individuals who have new and challenging ideas. The good reporter is the one who comes away from an interview with new knowledge, new ideas; in short, for the good reporter, interviewing is an educational experience.

Now, let us turn to problems inherent in interviewing and in dealing with the sources. The reporter has to gain cooperation of the source to obtain frank, accurate, precise answers. Special problems involved in this process can be categorized into three general areas.

First, how does one deal with the hostile news source? In news gathering some principals are hostile because the reporter often seeks information that does not cast them in the best light. As indicated in an earlier chapter, conflict is one of the strongest news appeals for mass man.

If one is asked to interview the city clerk who has been accused of embezzling $100,000, chances are great that the clerk is not going to be eager to talk. However, the reporter must get the clerk's responses to the accusation if he is to have a balanced story. It becomes a matter of credibility and intent.

The reporter must convince the source that he is there to give an objective report, not to try the case in the local newspaper. In dealing with the hostile source, it is necessary to show that a reporter is honest, has integrity and is open-minded. In short, the writer must convince the source that he is neutral and wants to get the source's side of the story. The trust which the source has in the reporter is dependent to a great extent on the past record of the newspaper or broadcast station. If the medium has established a reputation of being fair, most news sources will be less reluctant to talk.

Second is the problem of rigidity which often marks the beginning reporter's approach. The successful interviewer is flexible in working with a news source and uses common sense as a guide. If the source is reluctant to give a reporter information, or if he tries to move to "off the record" or "no comment" responses, the reporter must gently move the source back by asking about less controversial aspects of the event. Chances are fairly good that the source will warm up sufficiently to trust the reporter and talk openly.

If, however, the source continues to respond by saying "no comment," the reporter is advised to turn to a counseling approach and point out the risks of "no comment." Those two words connotatively communicate that either the individual is hiding something or that he is admitting the charges. Either way the source risks biased interpretations by the general public.

It is usually possible to convince a source that he should talk about a topic. The convincing comes primarily from assurance by the reporter that he is interested in presenting all sides to the issue. If the source simply refuses to talk, and if the information is essential to the balanced news story, the reporter has no alternative but to report that the source had "no comment." Such a statement is necessary because the public must be made aware that the reporter made the attempt to be fair.

And, third is the problem of the reporter who researches a topic and an interviewee and refuses to deviate from his preconceived notions. This reporter develops a list of questions and becomes a slave to it. Research is an absolute necessity but the reporter must listen for new angles, new leads and follow up on them.

Telephone Interview

Brief mention should be made of the telephone interview, an important tool for reporters because it is quick, convenient and economical. The telephone is particularly handy when factual information is needed. It is not as useful for feature stories such as profiles where face-to-face interviewing is best for detail, color and description.

As is true in any interview, the reporter should identify himself to the source and explain briefly and specifically what he wants to talk to the source about.

Taking Notes

Interviewees differ in their reactions to note-taking and/or tape recorders. Experienced news sources are seldom bothered, but persons not often interviewed may become ill at ease, especially when a tape recorder is used. A reporter should be prepared to discontinue note-taking or tape recording if they interfere with the interview process. A reporter should be prepared to take only a few notes or perhaps none at all.

In any case, the reporter must train his memory so that as soon as he is able, he can write down key statements. The interviewer must concentrate at all times and not become so absorbed in taking notes that he fails to hear what the source is saying.

Many reporters find a tape recorder time consuming when they reach the writing stage because of numerous playbacks. The reporter should take notes on key points even when using a tape recorder because the note-taking process helps organize the materials prior to writing.

Exercises: Chapter 6

1. Assignment: Write a news story using a summary lead in which you report the key points presented by a speaker who made an in-class interview. The story should be developed around a central theme with quotes and paraphrases presented to support the theme.

2. Assignment: Interview a student on campus who has been elected to a campus office or who has won an achievement award. Write a two-page interview story for the campus newspaper.

7

References for Journalists

Primary research is an important tool for the journalist, but those who want to communicate accurately and objectively in the 20th century must work with secondary or reference sources. Reference materials are available covering virtually every subject. With the emergence of the computer as a tool for information storage and retrieval, the parameters are almost limitless. This chapter presents sources of information used by media practitioners to research background on news, features, documentaries, advertising rates and circulation. There are 12 broad reference categories for the research-oriented reporter.

News Digests

News digests, as the name implies, present a compendium of news events categorized into sub-topics such as economics, government, religion, education, science and people. One group of digests deals exclusively with news events, one with comment and one with congressional and political activities.

Facts on File

This weekly digest of world news is published by Facts on File Inc., New York. News items are arranged under broad subject headings, and synopses and references to information on topics are presented. The publication has an excellent twice-a-month index that covers subjects such as Finance, Science, Economics, Education, Book Publishing, Religion, Obituaries of famous people.

Editorial Research Reports

Editorial Research Reports is issued four times a month by Editorial Research Reports Inc., Washington, D.C. It provides background articles of 6,000 words on significant regional, national and international topics. The service also publishes a number of short (250 to 500 words) articles on spot news developments. It is designed as an aid in developing editorials, columns and indepth articles. The publication summarizes previously published longer articles for those who have limited time.

Congressional Quarterly Weekly Report

Editors, reporters and news directors covering the federal government turn to the **Congressional Quarterly Weekly Report** for a digest of congressional and political activities. The publication, issued by Congressional Quarterly Inc., carries texts of major speeches and statements made in the U.S. Congress.

Fact Finders

Fact finders in the vernacular of the researcher represent compendia of facts and figures covering virtually every topic. Chief among the fact finders are two popular ones, **World Almanac** and **Information Please Almanac**. Both, as well as other recently issued almanacs, are used by reporters and editors to verify facts. **World Almanac,** typical of the publications in this category, has been called the most used reference book and foremost source of facts and figures. It has an excellent index and among its sections are a chronology of the major events of the year, population and election statistics, listing of senators and congressmen for each state, charts to show how each state has voted in presidential elections from 1932 to the present, statistics on major sports, economic data for major countries, listing of the winners of the Miss America and other contests, Academy Awards, etc.

Directories

Directories have evolved for most professions and industries. Five key directories are essential reference for personnel in the journalism and mass communication fields. Four are media oriented and the fifth is a government compendium.

Ayer's Directory of Publications

Ayer's Directory was first published in 1869. It is a general directory that covers U.S. and Canadian publications and is published by IMS Press. It contains a complete list of daily and weekly journals and newspapers published in the U.S. and Canada with names of the chief personnel. **N.W. Ayer's Directory** information is supplied by the newspapers and magazines, and the accuracy is dependent on the company responses. Each entry gives brief information on the town, the county, the population and the key industries. It contains limited information on advertising and circulation.

Editor and Publisher International Yearbook

This directory, issued annually by **Editor and Publisher** magazine, is the encyclopedia of the newspaper industry. It includes more than 250,000 facts about the U.S. and Canadian newspaper industry. It is alphabetized by state and by city, and entries give circulation, advertising rate, mechanical requirements, staff assignments and ownership of each daily newspaper. Sections exist on Syndicated Services, Wire Services, Group Newspaper Operations, Cross-Media Ownership, College and University Newspapers. Market information about trade territory population, city population, etc., for each city is listed.

Standard Rate and Data Service

This directory is filled with detailed information about markets served by newspapers, consumer magazines, radio, television, farm publications, general interest magazines, etc. A separate volume is issued for each of the categories. SRDS, as it is commonly referred to, is used by advertising agencies, space buyers, marketing specialists and journalists to obtain detailed information on advertising costs and reach.

Broadcasting Yearbook

Broadcasting magazine, like **Editor and Publisher,** issues an annual directory of the major units of the broadcasting industry. The book contains a directory of U.S. and Canadian radio, television and cable broadcasting stations, statistical tables on radio and television sales, listing of producers and distributors in the industry and market information.

Congressional Directory

This publication is issued every other year by the U.S. government; it gives detailed information about Congress, names of individuals and organizations associated with it, lobbyists, etc. It is a key reference for reporters and editors who cover the federal government.

Newspaper Indexes

Most major metropolitan newspapers publish a monthly index which is cumulated annually. A number of the newspapers have stored their publications on computer as a replacement for the hard-copy index. **The New York Times Index** is one of the oldest and most often used U.S. newspaper indexes. It is cited here because **The Times** is the closest the United States has to a national newspaper. The index is issued twice a month and a single volume is published at the end of the year. Major news stories covered by **The Times** with a brief summary are indexed; the listing includes obituaries and texts of important speeches and documents. It is especially good for checking the spelling of new nations, the accuracy of sports records, memberships of senate committees, etc.

Periodical Indexes

Research occupies much of the reporter's time. It, therefore, seems logical that he should be well versed in indexes which cover major articles published in scholarly, technical and popular journals. Journalists should become familiar with three basic periodical indexes: **Public Affairs Information Service (PAIS), Education Index** and **Readers' Guide to Periodical Literature.**

Public Affairs Information Services (PAIS)

This reference indexes a number of more specialized publications, especially those the reporter and editor would turn to for articles on public affairs. It is issued semi-monthly by PAIS and cumulative annual indexes are published. It can be used to search for articles on government, economics, mass communications, sociology, education, etc.; the publications indexed are scholarly or specialized. The front section of the book lists the publications that are catalogued; among those of special interest to journalists are **Editor and Publisher, Broadcasting, Columbia Journalism Review, Journalism Quarterly,**

Psychology Today and **Journal of Communications**. Articles are indexed alphabetically.

Education Index

This index is published monthly and cumulated annually by the H.W. Wilson Co., New York. It alphabetizes subjects as well as authors, and as the name implies, articles indexed usually have some link to education.

Readers' Guide to Periodical Literature

Readers' Guide to Periodical Literature is the general reference index used by most students for their first high school term paper. It is a general, all-purpose index that is cumulated annually by the H.W. Wilson Co. It includes subjects published in several hundred popular magazines and one can expect to find the articles written in the vernacular of the layman. Both subject matter and author indexes are used.

Biographical Sources

Most reporters and editors obtain biographical information on local, state and regional personalities from the newspaper's morgue or information storage system. However, numerous occasions call for the journalist to develop background on national and international personalities. Also, the copy editor may need to verify information on the background of an individual presented in a wire service or public relations release. Three biographical references are widely used.

Biography Almanac

Biography Almanac is a comprehensive reference guide to more than 20,000 famous and infamous newsmakers from Biblical times to the present as found in more than 300 readily available biographical sources.

Who's Who In America

Who's Who in America is widely used as a principal source for information on poets, authors, etc. It condenses biographies of 50,000 prominent living Americans, giving minimal facts supplied by the person. Entries give name, address, date of birth, family background, professional experience, articles and books published and organizations with which the individual is associated. It is published by Marquis Who's Who, Chicago.

Current Biography

The publication is issued annually by the H.W. Wilson Co. and includes brief articles on world news makers. It is limited to 350 names a year. In addition to the brief biographical information, the publication lists references to other biographical sources for the subjects. There is also a section of obituaries at the back of the volume.

The three biographical sources are rather exclusive, and when the journalist has need of information about lesser known individuals, he usually turns to one of the Who's Who Series. Published periodically by Marquis as well as others, the series includes educators, businessmen, leaders, etc., in Science, Social Science, the Southwest, South, Education, etc.

Dictionaries and Word Books

Language is the tool of the journalism profession, and the practitioner should have a thorough understanding of all aspects of English usage. Five commonly used references in this category are on virtually every editor's bookshelf. Two dictionaries predominate in the newsroom: **Webster's New International Dictionary** and **Webster's New Collegiate Dictionary**. Both are good all-purpose dictionaries and present language as it is used today. They present idiomatic and colloquial usage.

The word books that most journalists and writers use are **Roget's Thesarus** and **Thesarus II**. These books present synonyms grouped by ideas or subjects, and they have excellent indexes. A word of caution, the Thesarus should not be viewed as a source for obscure synonyms.

Many reporters will be assigned to cover the courthouse. When that assignment comes, it is imperative that one understand the language of the courtroom. It is not possible to commit all of the specialized terms to memory. A reference book that should be on the desk of those who cover public affairs, especially the courts, is **Black's Law Dictionary**, one of the best lexicons of legal terminology.

Like it or not, we live in a day of governmentese, and it is necessary for persons covering government to be able to decipher government acronyms and initials. An example is OSHA, the acronym for the Occupational Safety and Health Administration. The **Acronyms and Initialisms Dictionary** should have a place on the journalist's bookshelf. It provides a key to more than 45,000 acronyms with emphasis on American terms. A few foreign terms that are used widely in the United States are also included. The cover page for the book says that it is a guide to Acronyms, Initialisms, Abbreviations, Contractions, Alphabetic Symbols.

Quotation Books

The reporter and the copy editor often are called upon to verify literary, historical and other quotations used by speakers and writers, as well as to come up with the correct quotation for literary illusion leads. It's amazing how imprecise some speakers become when they borrow from great authors. There are two major sources for verification of direct quotes. **Bartlett's Familiar Quotations** is the most famous. Well known quotes (approximately 110,000) are arranged chronologically by authors. The publication also has an excellent keyword index. The other publication, similar in format, is the **Oxford Dictionary of Quotations.**

Local Directories

Three local directories are used extensively by journalists to check the accuracy of facts, spelling of names and other data ranging from home ownership to market data. A brief explanation of each is given below; the serious student of mass communication is urged to become acquainted with these publications. A good way to accomplish this is to go to the library and spend a few hours exploring city and telephone directories. The third source, the Reverse Telephone Directory, can be examined at a local newspaper or broadcast station.

City Directory

The publication is issued annually by a number of publishers. The compilation presents an alphabetical listing of names, family data (head of the household, spouse and children), home ownership, place of employment of adult members of the unit and often times religious affiliation. Because of recent concerns about invasion of privacy and reluctance of people to reveal information, the typical city directory no longer is as complete a tool as was true 10 to 15 years ago. However, it continues to provide an excellent checklist for reporting and editing personnel. Some city directories present a fairly comprehensive summary of the local city government, business district, educational system and a brief history of the town.

Local Telephone Directory

The local telephone directory contains numerous pieces of information helpful to the reporter and copy editor. It is readily available, and in most instances it is considered accurate. In addition to a listing of the names and addresses of individuals who have telephones, the directory contains the following information: background on the city and county, a rundown on the arts, the humanities and recreational and educational institutions in the city.

Reverse Telephone Directory

The reverse telephone directory is issued to businesses within a community. It organizes the city according to street addresses, not names, and usually there is an organization by consecutive order of telephone numbers. It is useful to the reporter and editor as a quick and efficient method to contact sources on a news event when only the address is known. For example, a fire call comes over the police scanner. It is at 229 S. Duck St. The radio station is on deadline for the 10 a.m. newscast. There's not enough time to get a reporter to the scene, but the station wants to get something on the air now. The reporter can use the reverse telephone directory to call people who live near 229 S. Duck to get information for the bulletin.

Yearbooks

Reporters and editors who handle public affairs news stories, features, indepth articles and editorials depend on a number of yearbooks for basic information about local, state, national and international leaders. Three yearbooks are briefly described below.

Statesman's Yearbook

The Statesman's Yearbook is an international yearbook that gives short, well-written summaries on political, economic, social, historical, educational, religious and military aspects of every country in the world. Its subtitle is "Statistical and Historical Annual of the States of the World." It is published by St. Martin's Press, New York.

The Book of the States

The Book of the States is a compendium that describes the governments of the 50 states. It is issued biannually by the Council of State Governments and contains a directory of state officials.

Municipal Yearbook

The Municipal Yearbook is published annually by the International City Management Association. It presents information, statistics and other directory information on cities in the United States and Canada.

Computer-Based Data Systems

In the computer age, virtually every day a new computer-based information system reaches the market. These computer-based systems have the capability of providing massive research materials almost instantaneously. Typical of the systems are the **New York Times** Information Bank and the Magazine Index.

Magazine Index

This service indexes some 372 of the country's most popular magazines and covers 1976 to the present. The computer retrieval system makes available information on evaluation of new products, review of books, movies, drama, TV shows, records, etc. A fee is charged for users of the service.

New York Times Information Bank

The Information Bank covers politics, economics, social problems and current affairs as reported in the late city editor of **The New York Times** and 55 other newspapers and periodicals. It is sold on a contract basis.

Books in Print

Access to information about books published in the United States is essential to the reporter and editor. Copy editors must be certain that titles of books as well as authors are correct. **Books in Print** and **Paperbacks in Print** are published by R.R. Bowker Co., New York. Each title comes in title and author volumes.

Exercise: Chapter 7

Assignment: verify the following information by using standard library references.

1. You have a client who wants to know how much it will cost him to place a full-page advertisement in (1) The Tulsa (Okla.) Tribune; (2) The Dallas (Tex.) Morning News; (3) The Minneapolis Star & Tribune; (4) The Washington (D.C.) Post. Get the information for him and tell the source of it.

2. What is the circulation of the daily newspaper published in your city or the city in which your university is located? Where did you find the information?

3. Who owns Channel 4-TV in Dallas, Texas? Source of information?

4. You are asked to do a short paper on the Electronic Newspaper. What index would you turn to for bibliographic entries? Go to that index and list three articles published in the past two years on the topic. Give author, title, publication, date, page documentation.

5. According to **Who's Who in America,** when was Katherine Graham born?

6. Here's a quotation: "These are the times that try our souls." Is this correct? Source of verification, and the correction if needed.

7. Who are the U.S. senators from your home state or the state in which your university is located? Source of information.

8. How did your home state vote in the 1980 presidential election? Source of the information?

9. Using sources other than the Card Catalog, show who wrote, painted or otherwise created the following:

The 95 Theses; Pygmalion; The Wealth of Nations; Swan Lake Ballet; The Aneid; The Steam Engine; Ivanoe; the Jungle; Madame Bovary; La Traviata. Specify the source of your information in each instance.

10. What is the cost of a 30-second spot to be aired over a major radio station in your hometown or the city in which your university is located? Source of the information.

Feature Writing

8

Straight news reporting is the bread and butter of journalism. But if all media content were hard news, there would be problems getting and holding an audience.

Editors such as James Gordon Bennett, Charles A. Dana and Horace Greeley early learned that laymen wanted to be entertained as well as informed. During the Penny Press Period (1833 to 1860), these journalism giants struck upon a writing formula that interested the average person. That formula was the feature story.

Earlyday journalists described their new-found writing style as creative, sometimes subjective, always entertaining, but also informative. The feature story still has a significant role. In this unit we will look at the feature story as a journalistic product, at types of features, types of leads used, where to find ideas for features and styles of writing.

Features Defined

As many definitions exist for features as there are editors and reporters. However, a good one is simple: feature articles are creative journalism. They are creative because the process involves creative thinking, research and writing. As in straight news reporting, most of the work in developing good features is thinking and research. The feature, too, may be subjective because it is often written as an indepth approach to the news.

A word of caution: when we say the feature is often subjective, we are not saying it is created by a reporter who sits down and spins a yarn off the top of his head. The good feature is based on factual information gleaned by the writer from research and interviews. Whether subjective or objective, the story is an experience for the reader/listener/viewer. It's an experience because the writer has developed keen insight into an issue, idea, event or person. The writer, through good language skills, presents the message so that the reader/viewer/listener vicariously experiences it.

With this definition in mind, let us turn to a hypothetical example of how a reporter might develop a feature. The creative stage refers to idea development, topic selection, conceptualization and brainstorming. Let's say an editor tells a reporter in mid-November that he wants a Christmas feature. The first step will be to brainstorm.

The reporter thinks about the topic: what approach can be used that will be unique, interesting, natural and yet capture the spirit of the season? Everybody has done the spirit of Christmas story, the commercialization of Christmas, interesting customs, trees, decorations, etc.

Perhaps a new approach could be an experiential feature. The experiential feature permits a reporter to experience an event and then write. A possibility would be get a job as a Santa Claus at a department store, listen to children requesting gifts, carefully observe the reactions of the children to Santa, the selfishness of some children. The reporter has a new angle or perspective from which to write.

Features can be creative and subjective and they also can be used in campaigns for change needed in a community. As an example, one college reporter became incensed because he could not find the required reading texts on library reserve. Librarians said the books were in use by other students in the building. After talking with students and observing that several had easy access to the books, he concluded that a small group was copping the books from the reserve room. Impossible, he was told.

To test the impossibility, he set out to prove that stealing books from the library was simple. Too simple. Dressed in coveralls, the young man went to the reserve room, picked up an armload of books, got on the elevator, got off at the basement level, walked across the unfinished basement, took the outside elevator to the first floor, left the building and put the books in a professor's office. He talked with the librarian about locating the reserve books. They were being used in the library, he was told. At that point the student asked the librarian to go to the office outside the buiding to get the books.

This scenario provided the seed for an excellent indepth feature on a form of academic dishonesty among students. The result was a planned observation story, an experiential story that called attention to a problem. It brought about changes in the processing of books in the reserve room. There's information, there's subjective comment and there's entertainment.

Experiential stories are good only if they can be developed around a theme that interests the audience. No idea can evolve as an effective feature if the article is nothing more than an ego trip for the writer.

Entertaining Features

Good features, for the most part, are entertaining and provide insight into people, events, ideas. One such feature is the color story, a side-bar or a side-trip into the interesting nooks and crannies of a news event. It paints pictures that show an event or person in detail.

A color story identified two or three "regulars" at all home football games. These people had sat in the same seats for 20 to 25 years and had not missed a home game. They had insight that helped a writer spin a yarn that kept the audience spellbound. The writer reported the oldsters' reactions to changes in the game, in the spectators, in players. The color story relies on descriptive word pictures which help the reader or listener know what it was like to have been there.

Feature Story Development

Reporters write stories that will fill space specified by an editor. They are reluctant to accept an editor's advice that a feature story should be as long as it can be kept interesting. To assign a given length to a feature is like telling an artist to use only three colors in his masterpiece. A basic yardstick in writing a feature is to write for reader interest. Length is secondary. . . interest in the topic is primary. Features may be two to three paragraphs or pages in length.

The feature story is effectively developed by plotting a theme around which to build the story. The theme is the central idea or the reason for a story's existence. It should be obvious. From the theme the writer develops specific questions to direct research and writing. In developing the feature, the writer comes to grips with three basic questions: (1) What is the best type of feature to tell the story?; (2) What type of lead should be used? and (3) What type of ending will close out the story to give it the feel of a piece of literature?

Types of Features

At least five types of features are used in the mass media. Each helps set a mood. A knowledge of the types of features will give the writer a foundation for sources of ideas.

News Features

A news feature is by definition an extension of a news story. It is a follow-up that presents color, depth, interpretation or new and unusual angles to a hard or soft news story.

By way of elaboration, let us establish a definition for hard and soft news. A number of years ago one of the foremost journalism educators, the late Frank Luther Mott of the Universities of Iowa and Missouri, categorized news as hard and soft. Hard news is spot news coverage about social, political, economic issues that provides the reader/viewer/listener a base of knowledge for decision-making. On the other hand, news that is entertaining, not essential for decision-making on significant issues, is soft news.

News features are built around news events, follow-ups that develop a specific angle. They have a strong timely angle and focus on the human interest elements related to the straight news event. For example, a reporter reads a news story that research by a noted psychologist shows that high school and college students are becoming addicted to soap operas. Soaps were originally thought of as directed toward the housewife who sought escape from the humdrum of homemaking. The story has news value because of the unusual angle or results. A good news feature could be developed around the theme of the psychologist's research. The reporter interviews a number of students who watch soap operas to see how prevalent the practice is, why soaps are so popular and any other pertinent details. Here we have an indepth news feature.

The number and scope of news features is limited only by the reporter's insight. Virtually every news story provides the beginning for a news feature.

Process Feature

The process feature can be a how-to-do-it or how-things-work story. How-to-do-it possibilities abound in every field, but they are not easy pieces to write. Most people find it difficult to write an explanation of routine tasks.

A good article could be developed about a local swimming pool outlet employee who bought a book on genealogy and using his home computer developed a program for family tree research that led to a new career. A how-it-works feature could be developed by a reporter to explain property assessments and functions of the tax collector's office. Stories that tell how something can be done simpler, cheaper and how something can be made easier to understand have a wide appeal.

Experience Feature

Experience features recount how someone achieved success or failure in business, hobbies, etc. They may also center on unusual personal experiences.

An experience feature was published recently about two housewives who tired of being housewives. They were excellent cooks. They did a market survey and discovered a demand for their expertise, and they opened a catering business. At first it was operated out of their home, then it grew. An enterprising reporter interviewed the women, used their journals and wrote an interesting and readable experience feature.

Personality Features

The personality feature is a word picture of the personality of an individual. In essence the personality feature is a painting that's built around strong human interest. Subjects for personality features need not be prominent; they need, however, to be newsworthy because of accomplishments, failures or events in which they have participated.

Every locality has thousands of subjects for this type feature. For example, a reporter went to a 50-year class reunion. He saw the name of a woman who received a B.S. degree in engineering. The reporter talked with her. She was the first woman to be graduated in engineering in the state...she had numerous anecdotes to tell about the problems she faced in a man's world. She is 75 years of age, has retired three times...is back in school to learn about computers because she wants a "mid-life" career in those new-fangled gadgets. The reporter came away with information for a phenomenal personality feature. It was a story that painted a word picture of the woman.

Information Feature

The information feature is usually lengthy because it develops background on a news event. Some call it the indepth or interpretive feature. It is becoming more prevalent in today's media; it updates the reader/viewer/listener on new and significant developments.

The information feature shows how an idea, an event or a concept has significance. As an example, let's say that the local hospital has purchased a body-scan apparatus. It rents for about $28,000 a month so the immediate reaction by the public may be that this is another way for the medical community to make money. The reporter can provide excellent service to readers/viewers/listeners if he talks with doctors, nurses and patients and writes a story that shows how efficient and successful the piece of equipment operates. If the device results in more precise diagnoses of dreaded diseases and earlier treatment, that's a story the public begs to have told.

Once the writer has come up with an idea for a feature, decided on the format it will take, he is ready to organize the story. Organization involves three basic units: the lead, the body and the ending. They must be tied together in a cohesive package.

The Lead

Leads for feature stories are based on concepts presented in an earlier chapter about straight news leads. The major difference in straight news leads and feature leads is one of style. Features are designed for the reader/viewer/listener who has time. They are leisurely done while straight news stories are brevity exemplified.

The lead is the key to writing a good feature story. Since the feature story is soft news and not crucial for reader, viewer or listener, the lead should perform two basic tasks: (1) draw the reader/viewer/listener into the story and (2) set the stage for the material that is to follow. The lead repertoire used by the writer is varied. He may use leads that startle and shock, that tickle the curiosity, stir imagination and inform. Seven basic rhetorical approaches (or lead types) are used by feature writers. Each is presented below with examples.

Summary Lead

The summary lead, as in straight news, gives the gist of the story, and it is used when the reporter has a strong, interesting subject. The summary emphasizes the most important "W or H" and in conversational tone prepares the reader/viewer/listener for the story. Here's an example:

> Jayne Smythe and Alice Watts are trying to beat the high cost of going to college. The two have pitched a tent in city park where they are paying $10 a month for rent. Both say that it's a little trying at times, but when they see their month-end checkbook balances, they forget about the inconveniences.

Narrative Lead

The narrative lead is a favorite rhetorical device of the fiction writer. It puts the reader into the story and draws him through it. The technique is to create a situation and skillfully involve the reader. The result of this is closely akin to a good movie which opens in the middle of the action. For example, the narration may cause one to become thirsty as the hero stumbles through the desert, or to tremble at the horror of a Frankenstein. Narration lends itself to longer stories because it takes time to build such a lead. Here's an example:

> Cold steel spikes pointed to a razor sharp loomed below as Adam Smythe's hands froze to the pipe that formed the framework for the construction-site elevator. A short 24 inches separated him from freedom and the outside world...twenty-four inches that seemed like a thousand feet. One slip and...well steel spikes make deep, intense cuts. Smythe set out to win a bet that he could escape from state prison and was stopped short as fear gripped his body.

An advantage of the narrative lead is that it can captivate the reader/viewer/listener better than any other lead style. Once the reader/viewer/listener identifies with the subject, he is hooked. The major disadvantage of the narrative lead is that few stories naturally lend themselves to this rhetoric. Reporters who try to force a narrative lead onto a story may find that the lead is either flat or unnatural, or that it distorts the story details.

Descriptive Lead

By definition, descriptive writing is designed to create mental pictures. It is especially applicable to the profile. It places the reader/viewer/listener a few feet away from the subject. The artful use of details that have universal meanings is the key to a descriptive lead. Descriptive writing makes the subject come alive...it permits the writer to create three-dimensional copy. Or it can be effective in bringing inanimate objects to life. Here are examples:

> His deep-set steel-blue eyes literally dance as he interrogates another 16-year-old drop-out brought in off the streets. The deep penetration of those eyes is like laser beams...the youngster's eyes dart back and forth as if programmed by one of the masterminds of a video game. Like a magnet, the 6-foot-four hulk of a man draws the teenager back. They are the eyes of a policeman, and he keeps his subject on target much like a king cobra mesmerizes a rodent as he sets the trap for a catch.
>
> * * *
>
> The laughter of children...the ringing of the bell to signal the start of classes...the tap-tap of the pointer on the edge of the shiny white oak desk seem to drift from the 75-year-old one-room school house that once was the social

and cultural center for the community. Now deserted, overrun by cockleburrs that thrive in the 108-degree blistering Oklahoma sun, still the school is revered by its former students and teachers.

Description in the hands of a good writer adds sparkle, but to be effective it must be concrete rather than abstract. Compare the two examples that follow:

The new Miss America is a pretty young coed who attends State University. (Abstract.)

The new Miss America's large brown eyes twinkled as she peeked from beneath blonde bangs... The State University coed wears no makeup because, "I don't have to rely on warpaint to attract men. And, even if I needed it, I wouldn't wear it." (Concrete)

Quotation Lead

The same admonition about direct quote leads that was presented on straight news applies to features. Occasionally the direct quote is the best and only way to begin a feature story. If the quote is profound and succinct, and the speaker is well known, it can give insight into the character of the subject. For a quotation to be effective, however, it must be strong enough that it sets the stage for the story to follow. That is, the quote must focus on the theme for the story. Here's an example of a good quote lead:

"Students, my friends, are a damned nuisance... but I wouldn't be deprived of that nuisance for a million dollars," growled one of State University's most admired and honored professors as he defended today's crop of students as among the " best prepared academically."

This quote gives insight into the person. It startles... it piques one's curiosity.

Question Lead

The question lead, like the quotation, can be effective if it isn't overworked. It must challenge the audience's knowledge or curiosity. There is a tendency among beginning writers, however, to cast leads as questions because they have the notion that the question sets the stage for the body of a story and makes writing simpler. The question lead that is merely a question is boring. Let's take an example of a story that effectively uses the question lead:

> Honesty is the best policy. Right?
> Wrong.
> Just ask Mack Doakes who lives in Podunk.
> Doakes was stopped last night by a burly man as he was returning from a movie. Said the man to Doakes, "Do you think I need a shave and a haircut?"
> Doakes surveyed the man who had a white stubble on his face and hair down to his neck.
> "Yes, I'd say you do, sir."
> Police found Doakes out cold. When he came around, he said that he guessed he had been too honest with his assailant.

Short, page brighteners often lend themselves to this treatment.

Direct Address Lead

The direct address lead is similar to advertising copywriting. In this style the reporter communicates directly to the reader. The lead says "this is for you and you alone." It makes use of personal nouns and pronouns. The direct address lead should be used sparingly. Here's an example of a direct address lead:

> So you think you're an ethical journalist? Chances are that you have violated the trust given to you as a professional several times today. That luncheon ticket you accepted from the Chamber of Commerce so you could cover the speaker's remarks. . . that press box ticket you accepted for last weekend's football game. The list is long. And your acceptance of these gratuities, while each seemingly is not big in itself, wears away at the objectivity in your journalistic performance.

Teaser Lead

The teaser lead is a device to "deceive" readers/viewers/listeners in a jesting manner. Its objective is to grab their curiosity and gently lead them into the story. Stories that use this approach generally are short, crisp, and light. It is similar to a suspended interest lead in that it gives little or no insight into the nature of the story. It is used extensively for page brighteners. Here's an example:

>Officer Joe Smith's ruddy complexion is no longer ruddy.
>
>Today, it's more a Rudolph-the-red-nosed-reindeer red.
>
>Smith walked to work yesterday afternoon. On the way there he did his good deed by helping a woman, about 65 years old, get her car started. She had battery trouble and the car required a push.
>
>Smith obliged her.
>
>As he was tidying up his desk to leave the night shift, officer Jones brought the same little lady into the precinct. Jones told Smith to book her for robbery.
>
>"Robbery?" Smith said.
>
>"That's right," Jones said. "She held up the Westside Cleaners this afternoon and got away with $5,000. We caught her when her car stalled on Sixth Street."
>
>'Yeah," the lady said, "they weren't as nice as you, sonny."

The Body of the Feature Story

The body of the feature story is best developed thematically. The reader/viewer/listener is introduced to the theme in the lead. The writer uses anecdotes, description, narration and quotations to weave the body of the story around the theme. He must make sure that all elements in the body support the theme and that he does not introduce non-related details. As mentioned earlier, a reporter must do a first-rate job of research. The end product should be a piece of writing that amplifies the lead and directs the reader through the story.

The feature format, unlike the straight news story, follows the style of the short story or essay. Material is presented in logical progression. The inverted pyramid is abandoned. The writer follows what might be called an inverted pyramid superimposed on a standard pyramid. Diagramatically, the feature can be presented as follows:

Diagram: Feature Story Organization

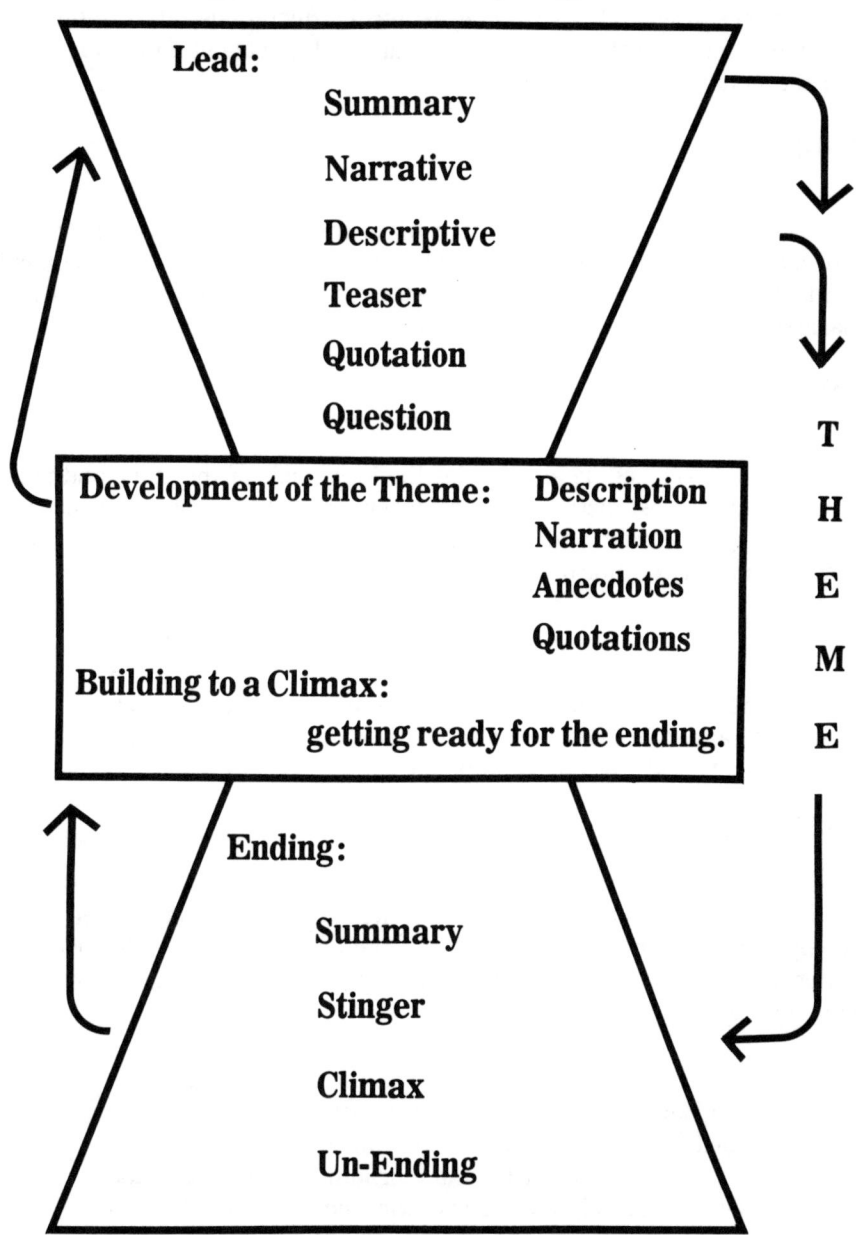

Lead:
- Summary
- Narrative
- Descriptive
- Teaser
- Quotation
- Question

Development of the Theme:
- Description
- Narration
- Anecdotes
- Quotations

Building to a Climax:
getting ready for the ending.

Ending:
- Summary
- Stinger
- Climax
- Un-Ending

THEME

The feature story presented on pages 102 to 104 illustrates the use of some of these factors. The student is urged to study the article to identify the stylistic devices used. The writer uses direct quotations, description and narration to develop the story. This is a feature that points out a problem, and it plays on the human interest angle strongly.

Endings

Most pieces of writing for the mass media have no formal ending. Feature stories demand a different treatment. Some are long by journalistic standards which creates a need to tie together loose ends. Writers use at least four basic styles of endings for feature stories.

Summary Ending

The summary ending simply ties the loose ends of the story and points back to the lead. In most instances the reporter restates the basic concept of the lead and through contrast and comparison leaves the reader/viewer/listener with a summary. An example of a summary ending follows:

> Perspiration dripped from Mack's forehead and trickled down his face. He mopped his brow with a handkerchief, stepped to the pool table, chalked his stick and aimed at the cue ball. The two corner balls hit the pockets, and Mack was champion.

Climax Ending

This type ending is popular in stories written in chronological order. It's closely akin to the traditional literary format except that in the feature story the writer stops at the point where the outcome of the story is clear. Here's an example of the climax ending:

> As the "sharks" entered the final round of the match, Mack, the champion, sank two balls to tie. Joe stepped to the table, aimed his stick and missed the shot.
> The time set for the tournament was in the last minutes. Hurriedly the judges refigured the score. A math error gave the match to Mack by one point.

The Stinger Ending

The stinger ending is a startling, surprising ending designed to jolt the reader/viewer/listener. Basically the writer uses an O. Henry-type ending. He sets up the reader/viewer/listener in the body of the story and throws him a curve, so to speak, with the unexpected conclusion. An example of the stinger ending follows:

> Perspiration dripped from Mack's forehead and trickled down his face. He mopped his brow with a handkerchief, stepped to the pool table, aimed at the cue ball. The corner balls missed the pockets. The champion had lost the match.

The Un-Ending Ending

In the un-ending ending the writer uses a style similar to modern TV programs. The copy hangs and leaves it to the reader/viewer/listener to provide an ending based on the information presented in the article. The writer purposefully ends by emphasizing a key, unanswered question wrapping up the story just before the climax. He uses this approach because the outcome isn't yet known, or because the writer simply wants to leave the reader/viewer/listener hanging. The un-ending ending is illustrated in the following:

> As the "sharks" entered the final round, Mack took aim on the cue ball and as sweat beaded on his forehead and trickled down his face, he went for the goal he had set before the match.

In this chapter we have looked at feature writing from different angles. The feature story offers the writer opportunities to be creative in writing and thinking. It provides the audience with neat packages of information in an entertaining manner.

By Susan Witt

RYAN—It was a blustery November night and Orvell White had settled into bed.

At 11 p.m. he was jolted from sleep by banging on the door of his trailer home.

"You're under arrest," a bail bondsman barked when White answered the door while struggling to pull on his pants.

"What for?" White asked.

He listened in dismay as two bondsmen told him he was wanted in Eufaula, 200 miles across the state, for jumping bond on charges of child abandonment and drunken driving.

"You've got the wrong man," White protested, explaining there were two men with the same name in the small Jefferson County town.

Besides, he said, he was a bachelor, a teetotaler and didn't even know where Eufaula was.

His relatives, who lived nearby, verified White's story and told the bondsmen the 45-year-old machine shop worker had never been in trouble in his life.

Nothing fazed bondsmen Mack Kelly and Gurnie Warenburg. "It just didn't seem to soak through their skulls," White said.

It has been seven years since White was jerked out of bed, handcuffed, hauled across the state and thrown into a "filthy" jail cell by bondsmen who confused him with another man.

White is still filled with anger when he thinks about the way he was treated by the men, who he says later tried to shrug off the mistake by offering him "a couple of hundred dollars" to forget it.

Officials say little can be done under Oklahoma law to prevent such abuses since practically "anything goes" when a bondsman arrests a bond-jumper.

"Bondsmen for years have broken into homes, roughed people up and even kidnapped people," says Tulsa Police Chief Harry Stege.

A Ryan lawman who was present when the bondsmen arrested White said they ignored indications that they might have the wrong man.

"Kelly paid no attention to the protests and told White to come on, they had a long trip to go," said Lloyd Kimbro, a Jefferson County deputy sheriff who helped the bondsmen locate White's home.

Kimbro said Kelly checked White's driver's license which showed that his birth date was different from the White listed in the charge, and that the man they were about to arrest spelled his first name Orvell, while the McIntosh County charge spelled the name Orville.

"Kelly said there probably was a mistake in the paper work and that he was the right one and was going to take him on," Kimbro said.

White said the bondsmen then handcuffed his hands behind his back and shoved him in a car.

"I had to sit on my hands all the way down there," White said.

"They stopped in Duncan to eat and they were going to take me in the restaurant in handcuffs, but I wouldn't go," White said.

He said the bondsmen finally agreed to let him stay in the car while they ate, but said they warned him, "If you try to run off, we'll shoot you in the back."

"I said don't worry about it, I'll be right here in the car because I ain't got nowhere to run," White said.

At Eufaula, White was finger-printed and jailed, despite his protests to officials there.

"It was a filthy jail," he said.

"I never had seen the inside of a jailhouse before. The bed was so filthy that I wouldn't even sit on it. I just curled up in a corner of the cold floor and tried to sleep there."

The next day, court officials discovered they had indeed jailed the wrong man, and White was released. His brother and sister-in-law, who had waited outside the jail all night, drove him home.

The bondsmen, he said, "tried to apologize and pay me off with a couple of hundred dollars."

"But I wouldn't take it. I already had made up my mind I was going to sue them.

"I said, 'You're going to pay for this,' and they just said, 'You won't get a thing,'" White said.

"I just made a mistake and we paid for it," Kelly says of the incident.

White filed a $300,000 lawsuit in U.S. District Court in Oklahoma City against the firm for which Kelly and Warenburg acted as agents.

He later agreed to settle the lawsuit for $5,000.

Kelly said the fact that White protested that they were arresting the wrong guy is not unusual.

"They'll tell you anything," he said.

"I was looking for an Orville Lee White who lived in a trailer house. In a little town like Ryan, Okla., you don't find two Orville Lee Whites, about the same age and both of them living in trailer houses.

"I guess I didn't check it far enough. It was just one of those bad mistakes a fellow makes."(**Used by permission, The Tulsa Tribune.**)

Exercise: Chapter 8

Develop a complete feature story of about 3 to 4 pages (600 to 800 words). In developing the feature, consider the following criteria:

LEAD: Does it interest the reader by attracting attention and guiding him into the story? Is the lead complete; promises no more than story can deliver? Does the lead express a central theme that is the basis for the story?

BODY: Flows smoothly and through quotes and paraphrases, description, analogy, narration, amplifies and develops the central idea expressed in the lead; movement from one aspect of an idea to another is accomplished through smooth transitions that show the relationship of each unit to the whole.

CONCLUSION: Brings story to a smooth stop by such devices as a re-statement of the lead, a summary of the message or an un-ending ending.

GRAMMATICAL STRUCTURE: Subject/verb agreement; spelling is correct; names are accurate; identification is accurate and complete; selection and use of the exact word to add impact.

RESEARCH: Through use of at least two interview sources, the writer demonstrates that he has done his homework on the topic; article developed in third person; no first person used; demonstrates full knowledge of subject; article is built around information gleaned from primary and secondary sources, not merely re-hash of an experience that one has had or an off the top of the head presentation of one's ideas and opinions on the topic.

9

Advertising: the Support System

Advertising, like the telephone company is ubiquitous. Nobody escapes the impact of so-called Madison Avenue hucksters. Advertising is the life-line for the mass media industries. Were it not for the revenue produced through advertising and commercials, newspapers, magazines, radio and television as we know them would not exist in America. The typical U.S. newspaper derives some 80 percent of its income from advertising, while the typical radio or television station depends on commercials for approximately 90 percent of its revenue. The consumer is bombarded with jingles, psychological appeals and messages that he often sees as juvenile. Commercial messages do take up a large share of the time and space in the media. Advertising space in most newspapers averages 60 percent or more and about one-third of broadcast air time is commercials.

Advertising provides numerous benefits to society: lifeblood of the mass media, vitality to the economic system and information to help the consumer make rational and wise purchases. Advertising provides information about new products, products that make tasks easier, and competitive pricing and where the best buys are available. Its acceptance has helped make possible mass production. The argument can be advanced that advertising has contributed to raising the American standard of living. Advertising is part of the marketing system of the modern corporation, and there will always be demand for creative people who can plan, research, write and execute effective advertisements.

Advertising is communication that helps to sell products and build confidence in companies and institutions. Or said another way, it is useful, relevant and pertinent information upon which the consumer either acts immediately or stores for later reference, application or use. Advertising exemplifies the basic concepts of communication theory. For it to be effective there must be a linkage between the message sender and the message receiver, and the copy must be planned and written with the consumer's needs in mind.

Social critics have a heyday evaluating advertising. Positive as it may be for providing the lifeblood for the media industries and for helping the successful marketing of products, the field is viewed as a plague by many. Six basic themes characterize the criticism.

First, because advertising is pervasive, some people believe that it leads consumers to purchase things they do not need. The critics charge advertising is a hypnotic force which directs consumers.

Second, the critics say that advertising appeals to emotions rather than intellect. The messages emphasize emotional needs rather than concrete information about how a product works, what it is made of and what it will do. The complaint can be viewed as valid because advertising copy by its nature is communication that appeals to the consumer's needs.

Third, laymen tell us that advertising is biased...that there is no objectivity in the copy. Most advertising is directed to present a particular product or brand name in a favorable light. Highly subjective approaches are to be expected because the ultimate goal is to create sales. The merchant who pays the bill directs his advertising messages to bring prospects to his business to buy his products. He is subjective.

The fourth complaint says advertising involves conflicting claims. The copywriter picks up on the strong points of a particular brand and tells the consumer that another brand lacks the convenience or the effectiveness. An analysis of the copy reveals that the message is truthful; copywriters for competing brands emphasize different points.

A fifth criticism is that much of advertising is vulgar, obtrusive and irritating. For example, some say television and newspaper advertising for personal feminine products is not in good taste. Ads can be obtrusive because they interrupt the continuity of a TV drama, or they take up space that the critic feels should be devoted to coverage of significant hard news. As for advertising's being irritating, most copy writers say that repetitive and sometimes irritating copy drives a point home and helps to imprint the product upon the consumer's mind.

The final complaint—that advertising is unduly repetitive—is partially true. It is repetitive but for reasons. Market research and psychological studies tell us that repetition is a key aspect in learning, thus ad copy writers use repetition to drive their messages home. Repetition is part of the process of education.

This review of advertising criticisms shows that excellent research, writing and creative strategy are essential for success in advertising. It is a type of communication whose results can be tested quickly as the merchant checks his sales of items advertised.

The Advertising Process

The preparation of advertising messages can be divided into three basic processes: research and planning, visualization and writing. Each of the steps contributes specificity to the advertising campaign. The writer should go through a comprehensive analysis of the product and the customer to come up with strategy for executing the sales message.

Most beginners find that the 5 Ws and H provide an outline for copywriting. One of the first tasks for the copywriter is to define who is the specific audience for a product. The more specific the definition, the more direct the copy message. The who should be defined in terms of demographics as well as psychographics. Demographics present basic market data such as age, sex, occupation, income, education, types of family units, size of households, two-family income, etc. Psychographics, on the other hand, are the psychological extensions of the demographics. That is, psychographics involve such habitual attributes as life-style, personality traits, etc. Once the writer has identified the who, he can target his copy more accurately.

The what helps the writer to specify the product or service. The writer identifies the specific selling points of the product. The message may emphasize performance, convenience and work-reduction aspects of the product. Copywriters develop a unique selling proposition as they elaborate on the specific attributes of the product.

Identifying the prospect and the key selling points of a product represent a first step in the copywriting process. The other Ws and H can be used to enhance these factors. For example, where a product is available, both geographic and by store type, can provide background information to enhance the sales pitch. The when can be an important element in ad copy and is used primarily to tell consumers about seasonal buys. If one is selling seasonal products, the approach must stress immediacy of purchase or action.

When the copywriter turns to analysis of the why of a product, he is zeroing-in on the psychological aspects of advertising. From this analysis will come answers to such questions as why should a customer buy this specific product? Or put another way, what are the benefits the consumer will gain by buying at a particular store? One must remember that the U.S. consumer is a selfish individual; he is interested in "what's in this for me?" In this analysis, the writer turns to man's basic psychological needs: parental desire, sex desire, security desire, health desire, comfort desire, merriment desire, sociability desire, beauty desire, mastery desire and food and drink desire. These needs form the nucleus of an advertising appeal. An appeal is the stimulus used by the advertiser to get his message across to the audience.

After the copywriter has analyzed the audience and the product, he is ready to design the advertisement and to write the copy. The basic goal is to select the product's most important consumer benefit and feature it in a message that communicates quickly, clearly and completely.

Copy Approaches: Factual

Two basic copy approaches are used in retail advertising: factual and emotional. The copywriter should become acquainted with each and the styles used in developing them. Factual copy is rational and direct appeal copy. It emphasizes product information, reasons with the customer and focuses on qualities of the merchandise. Factual copy appeals to people who are conscious of a need for a product and who have already visualized the benefits they will derive. Five types of factual copy predominate in retail advertising.

Descriptive or Explanatory Copy

As the name implies this type presents straight-forward description of the product, or it explains the product's features. Product benefits predominate. It has been described as simple, straightforward, lay-it-on-the-line copy. Here is an example:

> Our classic collection of casual shirts do sensational things for your wardrobe...and your pocketbook. They come in color-fast cottons and in styles and shades that say welcome to autumn. Choose Polos and Izods in stripes and solids...coordinate with trousers or skirts. Wear them day or night. Sizes S,M,L,XL. $25 and up.

Reasons Why Copy

Using this approach, the writer presents logical copy. There is no emotion involved. The copy tells the customer why he should buy a particular product or why he should shop at a specific store. It may also emphasize how an item is best used and why the product meets the reader's needs. It emphasizes customer benefits and may utilize the direct address approach. Here's an example:

> It Makes Sense to Shop at Goetz...(headline)

Goetz is the place for back-to-school shoppers. Goetz has what YOU want. You get superb selection because we're a complete department store...more than 20 departments...all under one roof. Conveniently located...and ample free parking. You'll find everything to send your family back to school. At Goetz, the family store.

Promise Copy

In this type, the writer poses a problem that is common among typical customers. The copy then makes a promise that if one uses the product the problem can be solved quickly and efficiently. It is a stimulus to move customers to buy. It poses a problem and lets the advertisement present the answer. This approach can draw prospects toward a product. The ad copy below is an example:

Goetz's easy payment plan makes outfitting your family for school as simple as ABC.

It's easy. Come to Goetz...select your family's back-to-school clothing and school supplies...and just say "Charge It." And there's no payment due until September 30. Take 90 days to pay...without service charge. Goetz...we help you stretch back-to-school dollars

Testimonial Copy

Testimonial copy presents the key message about a product by letting a user relate benefits. It is especially convincing if the person making the testimony is widely known or possesses characteristics with which the consumer identifies. In the copy below note the conversational tone in the direct quotes from the user:

Why Housewives Like Shopping at Goetz

It's a great place to shop because Goetz clerks are friendly and helpful. You can find every item you need for back-to-school...Goetz stocks the largest clothing inventory in a three-state area. And, the prices are always right. Add to these the 90-day-like-cash purchase plan...You'll enjoy shopping at Goetz.–Mary Smith.

Performance Tests

This approach is commonly used in national advertisements in which the generic rather than the specific product is presented. The copy emphasizes results of product testing that prove that the item is the best on the market. Ad copy that emphasizes the **Good Housekeeping** Seal falls into this category as does directly quoted material from independent testing laboratories such as **Consumer Reports.** The copy below is an example:

> Tests determine quality: scientific tests, use tests. Sooner autos are subjected to rigid mechanical tests long before they arrive at your dealer's showroom. All mechanical parts are subjected to performance tests by our engineers... before the parts go into our cars. And an independent testing laboratory torturously tests the performance of our cars and gives its seal of approval... before our name goes on. Sooner... tomorrow's car today.

Emotional Copy

The second major category of advertising copy is emotional. In this approach the writer focuses almost exclusively on how the user will enjoy the product. It does not detail specific attributes; instead it presents the psychological enjoyment or social prestige that comes from using the product. In emotional copy the copywriter uses description. The approach has been called imaginative or creative because it concentrates on word images developed through warm, personal words. As an example, emotional copy writers sell "a look rather than clothes," "feet that feel warm in winter and free in summer rather than shoes," "home, comfort, prestige, security rather than a house."

Three basic types of emotional copy used in the advertising profession are presented here.

Narrative Copy

In typical narrative copy, the message is presented through the story-teller's mode. It is often patterned after classical literature, history, the fable or the fantasy. The writer attempts to put the key message in the mouths of fictitious characters and may use literary license to force the style to mesh with the literary pieces to which he alludes. The advertisement presented below makes use of the narrative or story-telling approach.

> Once upon a time in an Oriental province lived a king of the automobile clan. King of Auto was a so good that he gobbled up the American car industry. Everywhere one saw his Oriental Deluxe. King was ruler of the auto world...his subjects worshipped him because the O-Deluxe was the only economy car around. King's sales soared...he was so secure he gave the public the same car year after year.
>
> Meanwhile in a little-known hamlet in the central United States, a young auto Prince brought out his first car. Not much attention was given to Sooner until the word spread of its economy, its style, its comfort. Soon auto buyers demanded the Sooner...not Oriental Deluxe. But King was not concerned...he was king.
>
> Sooner continued to develop a better car...designed to meet U.S. Driver's special needs. Then one day the auto industry declared the King dead...Sooner quietly assumed the leader's position...but it continues to listen to the driver's special needs.

Dialogue Copy

In this approach, the writer phrases his copy as if two people were talking. To be effective, dialogue copy must be cleverly done, it must ring true, and it must sound the way real people talk. Dialogue copy often lets prospective customers ask questions, pose situations and lets the advertiser through copy present answers. The copy below is an example:

> (The first of three men pictured in a Sooner car ad).
>
> All I've got to say is that a car just isn't a car unless it offers comfort and economy...plenty of room to stretch without bumping my head...seats that are plush and soft to make riding a joy. And it must go easy on my pocketbook.
>
> (Car dealership speaks).
> Right you are...Comfort and economy...the Sooner was designed with you in mind. The Sooner seats 5

passengers comfortably...plenty of leg and headroom...and it gets 52 miles to a gallon...That's economy. And it comes in all colors...even in a sports model. See General Auto for your dream car today.

Predicament Copy

Often the ad writer develops copy by presenting a problem or a predicament and then a logical, efficient and easy solution. In this approach he lets the copy become a counselor. This is an especially good approach for institutional or item-selling copy. It is informal, conversational writing with emphasis on the consumer's interests. Such an approach is effective because it provides immediate reduction of anxiety for the consumer. Here's an example:

Got the old gas station blues?

Most everybody these days has problems with rising costs...with the cost of gasoline at $1.30 a gallon, your gasoline dollar is shrinking. Most gas guzzlers can hardly pass a service station.

There's good news for you from Sooner.

The new models feature an improved motor design that stretches your auto dollar. Engineering developments have produced a motor that purrs down the road at 55 mph...and it gets 52 miles to the gallon. So if you want to ring out the gas station blues...drop in at General Auto and get your Sooner today...it's your key to economy and comfort.

Exercises: Chapter 9

1. Study the market data on the all-electric car–the Asanuma. Write copy for an advertisement using one of the following approaches:

FACTUAL COPY–Use any of the types of factual copy presented in the textbook.

EMOTIONAL COPY–Use any of the types of emotional copy presented in the textbook.

You must write 180 words of copy to fill the ad layout–no more, no less.

COPY OBJECTIVE: State precisely what your objective is for the copy: to whom directed (age, sex, economic level, etc.); Is the copy and ad designed to introduce a new product? To encourage greater use of an existing product? What advertising appeals are you using? What psychological, wants or desires are you building your ad around?

THE PRODUCT: General Auto Co. has just developed a new car, the Asanuma. It's an electric automobile; seats 4 passengers comfortably. Powered by batteries that automatically recharge themselves using solar energy. In test drives the cars were driven consistently at 55 mph. No limitation on distance one can travel (that has been a problem with previously developed electric cars because batteries had to be recharged after 40 or so miles) because the batteries are re-charged by solar energy as you drive your car. The car sells for $16,000 and should last indefinitely. It has no movable parts in the engine to wear out, the body is made of fiberglass. The company says the car should cost approximately 25 cents a mile to operate–that's compared with 50 cents a mile it currently costs to run a conventional car. Car comes in a range of colors: black, gray, red, white, sand, green; can be ordered in two-tones as well as with a sports package. Two-tones and sports packages, of course, are optional equipment and cost extra.

2. Using the same information and instructions given in Assignment No. 1 above, prepare copy for a 60-second radio commercial. The delivery rate for the copy is 144 words a minute. Plan introduction and ending timing in doing the spot ad.

# 10

Public Relations

Public relations is a growing, dynamic field concerned with creating or maintaining a favorable image for a company or organization. Its practitioners spend much of their time crafting mass media messages. Therefore, it is important for those in PR to understand how the media work and how to write for the media.

Public relations can involve a wide range of duties and activities. The emphasis in this chapter is on what public relations is and how writing for media is related to public relations. Unfortunately, many beginners are not aware of the importance of strong media writing skills.

Public relations is important for all levels of government, business, military, law enforcement, education, and it includes activities ranging from writing press releases to producing documentaries and books. Public information is a vital function in our society because all institutions must inform other segments of society about their practices.

A basic rule of effective public relations is that organizations should provide--not hide--information about their activities. This philosophy is necessary for the PR practitioner

Communication Theory and PR

The public relations practitioner needs a thorough grounding in communication theory. The basic communication model of source-message-channel-receiver helps the beginner grasp the importance of each step in the communication process. A model reduces the complicated procedure and increases understanding.

One task of the PR person is to define the target audience--or to know who the intended receivers are. The target audience may be the public at large, a group of consumers, residents of a particular city or employees of a single company. The PR person must have the audience clearly in mind before beginning the job of constructing a message.

Determining the exact public and its wants and needs involves extensive research. In any case, the PR person who does not have a basis for what he does may find his messages are ineffective because they are not reaching the right people.

A second task of the PR person is to select the proper channel to reach the desired audience. The more that is known about the audience, the easier this task becomes. Media aimed at highly specialized audiences—such as subscribers to special-interest magazines—may be best for some releases. A general circulation newspaper or television news program may be best for releases to a broader audience.

Television is a dramatic medium which combines sound and visual appeal. The audiences are huge and messages have high impact and immediacy. On the other hand, newspapers and magazines allow for more depth and detail, and they are often read by older, better-educated people. A major function of the PR person is to construct messages that will convey what is intended to the receivers. If the message is unclear, ambiguous, misleading or difficult to decipher, it will not do its job.

Writing the PR Release

The role of the PR practitioner involves a wide range of functions as mentioned earlier. But one major function is writing for the mass media.

Earlier chapters have discussed techniques of writing straight news and feature stories. The PR person must be trained in these journalistic skills because they are the techniques of writing PR releases as well.

It is a mistake to assume that releases for the mass media should be written in some special "public relations" style. They should be written to emphasize news characteristics as explained in chapter 2. Editors are extremely sensitive to releases that try to masquerade as news. Most of those are thrown out. Releases that do not follow basic journalistic writing style are also dismissed as too much trouble. Busy editors don't have time for rewrites.

The PR person should maintain personal contacts with media personnel, and plan releases around deadlines. A news release that arrives after the deadline will not be used. Deadlines vary from medium to medium, and from area to area. They change often; therefore, the PR person must constantly check with the news media to anticipate and meet their needs.

The news release for print and broadcast should be easy to read, and written in the appropriate style and clearly marked. All of the rules of readability—short words, sentences, paragraphs—apply just as they do for practicing journalists.

Most news releases, especially for newspapers, are in the inverted pyramid format and should not be too long. A broadcast news release should usually be limited to 70 to 140 words that can read in 30 to 60 seconds. Print releases can be longer, but seldom exceed two or three pages.

Copy should be typed, double spaced with wide margins with a name and phone number of the PR person on the release. The PR writer must make sure facts are right, that names are correct and that proper style, grammar, spelling and punctuation are used. Mistakes can ruin one's credibility. A PR person who becomes a trusted news source for the media will find more of his releases being used.

The PR person should be helpful on calls from the media about news stories. The news media cooperate fully with PR persons they trust and who are cooperative with them.

The news release is a public statement about an organization or institution written in journalistic style. The news media and PR persons work together despite some inevitable tension about their roles. Many of the stories carried by the news media originate as PR releases, and PR persons contribute to many other stories by answering questions from the media.

The PR persons should not neglect the visual possibilities to go with releases. Photographs are useful for newspapers, magazines and television. Slides, illustrations, charts and other kinds of artwork might also be useful.

For an example of a PR release, the reader is referred to Appendix E.

Exercises: Chapter 10.

I. Write a 200-word release for local newspapers based on the following:

Assume you are the public relations director for the Middletown public schools. You are asked to write a news release based on the following:

The school superintendent is John Mills. He tells you that the state Department of Health has just completed a study of all city schools. The study was to determine if asbestos materials had been used in any of the school buldings. The Environmental Protection Agency considers asbestos to be a health hazard. The study reveals that some asbestos ceiling materials were found in the Middletown High School auditorium. No asbestos materials were found in any other schools or in any other areas of Middletown High School. There are 20 elementary and secondary schools in Middletown. The superintendent says it will cost $50,000 to apply sealant to the auditorium ceiling to correct the situation. He says he will ask the school board to authorize funds for the project. The board meets next Tuesday at 8 p.m. The project should take about two weeks to complete, the superintendent says. The superintendent said: "We are concerned about this. We want to correct this as soon as possible. We don't want anything in the schools that might affect the health of Middletown students."

II. Use the information in I above and write a news release of no more than 100 words for local radio and television stations.

III. Assume you are the public relations director for Williams Department Store, 101 N. Main St., a major retailer in your city. The president and owner, John Williams, asks you to send a 150-word news release to local newspapers. He is the source and he tells you the following:

"Williams Department Store will undergo a change which will be a great benefit to customers beginning Jan. 1. Williams will concentrate on retail specialization by discontinuing some lines. We will no longer sell major household appliances, hardware items or automobile parts. These departments will be closed out to enable us to devote more efforts to wearing apparel and linens. We will be able to make savings which will be passed on to customers. The areas to be closed now employ about 20 people, and these loyal workers will be moved to other departments of the store. We anticipate no layoffs because of this move. We built our reputation originally in soft goods—mainly clothes—and we are returning to that basic commitment. This is another effort by Williams Department Store to meet the needs of the citizens of our fair city."

IV. Use the information in III above and write a release of no more than 75 words for local radio and television stations.

11

Editing Media Copy

Editing is the third major step in the processing of news and information. News gathering and writing are the first two. A media reporter and writer performs the first step in editing on print and broadcast copy before he turns it into the desk. But all experienced news workers know that every writer's copy needs to be edited by someone else. At times this can be uncomfortable and disagreeable, especially for the sensitive young reporter who thinks his copy is above reproach. Seasoned journalists understand and welcome the necessary changes produced by editing.

Editors and news directors evaluate the news, decide how stories are played on a page or in a newscast and direct the news gathering efforts of their staffs. These are important management and decision functions of the news process. The emphasis in this chapter, however, will be on the techniques of the copy editor—the person who shapes, trims, polishes and improves news stories. The copy editor is the last person to handle a story in the chain before it reaches the reader or viewer.

A copy editor must have a broad understanding of local, national and international events. He must have knowledge of social, economic and political problems and procedures. He is called upon daily to decide which stories, which facts, which statements, which words or images are passed on to the news consumers. He must know the interests and needs of his readers and viewers.

In addition, editing calls for a keen awareness of grammar and syntax, of clarity, conciseness and accuracy in the use of language. The primary function of editing is to assist readers and listeners to understand the news quickly and easily. If this goal is accomplished, the editing process is successful.

The copy editor should read a story at least three times. The first time is a quick scanning to get the gist of the story; the second involves detailed line-by-line, word-by-word editing; and the third is to check to see that the story reads smoothly after editing changes.

The editor checks the story for readability. Numerous research studies indicate that short sentences and paragraphs are easiest for readers. An average sentence of 17 to 21 words seems to be most readable, and a spot news story paragraph should have no more than three sentences. Many newspaper paragraphs are one and two sentences.

The copy should be checked for accuracy. Readers and listeners quickly lose confidence in editors and broadcasters who make errors in news reports. In all newsrooms there is a daily battle to keep out mistakes. This means checking names, dates, ages, addresses, figures and other details. Often the story is returned to the reporter to check questions. Sometimes the editor must use reference materials in the newsroom. Those references were discussed in Chapter 7.

Basic reference sources widely used on the copy desk are the newspaper or broadcast station's morgue or library, dictionaries, atlases, almanacs, city directories, telephone directories, the U.S. postal guide, Congressional Directory and other sources such as various Who's Who publications.

The editor must check the story for internal consistency and accuracy. If the lead says three persons died in a fire, but there are four named as dead lower in the story, obviously the reporter has made a mistake.

Editing Words

Words are the primary tools of mass media writers and editors; therefore, they should be used with precision, care and understanding. An editor must have a broad and deep vocabulary, a high sense of word meaning and an appreciation and awareness of the language.

To communicate with a mass audience, simple, direct and easy-to-understand words are needed. Abstract, complex or technical words should be used rarely, and when they are used should be explained in simple terms. Readability tests show that Anglo-Saxon words of a few syllables are easiest to read. The editor should be alert to eliminate pompous, overblown and flowery language.

Some frequently misused words are listed here, and the reader is referred to Chapter 4 for a comprehensive list of common writing mistakes. There are many others that cause problems, and the alert copy editor will keep a dictionary handy at all times.

Accept, except—Accept means to receive; except means to leave out or exclude.

Aid, aide—Aid means to assist, and aide is a person who serves as an assistant.

Among, between—Between should be used when writing about two items, and among is used with three or more.

Anticipate, expect—Anticipate means to act in preparation for something; expect means to look forward to, but does not include the notion of preparation.

Capital, capitol—Capital refers to the city; capitol is the building.

Council, counsel—A council is a deliberative body of some type; counsel means advice or to advise.

Dived, dove—Dived is correct. Do not use dove for past tense of dive.

Farther, further—Farther refers to distance; further refers to time or degree.

Hangar, hanger—A hangar is a building for airplanes, and a hanger is used for clothes.

Majority, plurality—A majority means more than half of an amount; a plurality is more than the next highest number, but less than a majority.

Stationary, stationery—Stationary means to stand still and stationery means writing paper.

Editing Sentences

The copy editor must have a keen ear—and eye—for a smooth, well-constructed sentence. A good sentence is one that moves the news story along, offers information quickly and clearly and is easy to read. Nouns and verbs are the key ingredients; adverbs and adjectives are used sparingly because they are more connotative and slow or confuse the reader.

Facts, details, quotes pertinent to the story, chosen and written by an experienced journalist and polished by a well-trained editor, form the best sentences. The verbs should be strong and vigorous, and the nouns precise and accurate. Many—not all by any means—news sentences are simple, declarative sentences following the basic order of subject, verb and object. Some complex and compound sentences are necessary for variety, transition and emphasis.

A basic problem in editing is to make the sentences—and the story—concise. General wordiness is a frequent barrier to readability and understanding. Brevity and conciseness are followed by good news writers. Cliches, trite expressions, redundancies and clutter words and phrases should be edited.

For example, the following sentences can be improved by eliminating unnecessary words. Facts and details are not cut, only excess verbiage.

The policeman kept an eye on the black-colored car which was parked at the curb beside the street.

The policeman ~~kept an eye on~~ *watched* the black~~-colored~~ car which was parked at the curb.

The mayor is a man who in a short period of time reduced the total operating budget of the city.

The mayor ~~is a man who~~ in a short ~~period of~~ time reduced the ~~total operating~~ *city* budget ~~of the city~~.

The present incumbent congressman put in an appearance at the meeting of the City Council.

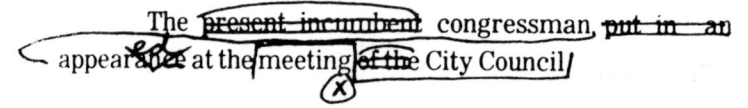

The ~~present incumbent~~ congressman ~~put in an~~ appeared at the meeting ~~of the~~ City Council.

Smith made good his escape from the jail.

Smith ~~made good his~~ escaped from the jail.

Active Voice

Generally, active voice is better than passive voice:

Smith called for an increase in taxes. (Active).
An increase in taxes was called for by Smith. (Passive).

The first sentence is more direct and more forceful. The passive voice is acceptable and even necessary when the emphasis in the sentence is to be placed on the object. If the tax increase were the most important element in the example above, the passive voice would be preferred.

The following example illustrates the use of active voice:

> The team lost the ball in the final seconds of the game. (Active).
> The ball was lost in the final seconds of the game by the team. (Passive).
> The senator delivered the speech. (Active).
> The speech was delivered by the senator. (Passive).

Faulty Construction

The structure of the sentence should help the reader grasp its meaning. The way words are arranged in the sentence should show their relationships, and one rule of clear writing and editing is that related words should be together. Modifiers should be as close as possible to the words they modify. The dangling modifier is a common, and often comical, mistake:

> Looking out the window, an airplane was seen. (The airplane was looking out the window? Probably not.)
> While walking into the library, a book was dropped by the professor.
> (Write it: The professor dropped a book while walking into the library.)
> The man confessed setting fires to police. (Write it: The man confessed to police that he set the fires.)

The rule of parallelism states that similar elements in a sentence should be in similar grammatical form. This example would not be parallel:

> He said he likes fishing, hunting and to ski. (One correct form would be: He said he likes fishing, hunting and skiing.)

The editor should see that the sentence has the proper emphasis, that first things are first. The most newsworthy elements should come first in the newspaper story sentence. Beginning reporters often back into the news with wordy phrases and clauses.

At 191 N. Main St., today, a fire killed three people.

Better: Three people died in a fire today at 191 N. Main St.

By a vote of 9-2 Thursday, the City Council approved construction of the new park.

Better: The City Council approved construction of the new park by a vote of 9-2 Thursday.

Editing Stories

The lead should be appropriate in tone, content and structure for the story. If the story is straight news, the lead should be a concise summary and the story structure should be the inverted pyramid. A feature or an analysis might require a different form.

The lead must be accurate, saying no more and no less than the facts support. The editor should make sure that interesting and important elements of the story are placed high. This means the lead is subjected to close scrutiny because the lead determines the success of the story. A weak, wordy, cluttered or inappropriate lead detracts from a story.

After the lead is edited, the editor moves into the body. He checks to see that the story is complete, accurate and answers questions the reader might raise. He also checks grammar, spelling, punctuation and style throughout the story. Notice how the following story was edited:

~~Officials said today that~~ three oilfield workers *today* were killed and four injured near Weston ~~when a storage~~ *natural gas* tank ~~which was used for natural gas blew up and~~ exploded, *officials said.* ~~The chief of police for~~ Weston *police chief* Mike Shorter said, ~~about two hours following the blast~~ the bodies of the three ~~killed oilfield workers~~ were found *two hours after the blast.*

(-more-)

The 400-barrel tank was ~~completely~~ destroyed ~~in the blast.~~ Several nearby tanks ~~in the surrounding vicinity~~ were in danger of exploding, ~~because of the heat from the fire~~, officials said.

Shorter said the ~~fire and~~ explosion occurred when workmen were welding a ~~flare~~ line which vents gas from the tank.

—30—

12

Basic Legal Concepts

The mass media writer needs a knowledge of basic legal concepts as they relate to communication. Libel and privacy are particularly troublesome.

Libel

The First Amendment states that Congress shall make no law "abridging the freedom of speech, or of the press. . ." The rationale behind the First Amendment was to ensure that government would have no censorship or prior restraint over publishing. But the press could be held accountable after publication for certain things. One area that the courts have consistently held the press accountable for has been libel. The press could be sued and forced to pay damages to a plaintiff who could prove libel.

To have an understanding of libel, a brief definition is needed. Basically, libel is a publication which holds a person up to hatred, ridicule, contempt, loss of esteem, humiliation, or damages them in their trade or profession. Libel laws differ somewhat in the 50 states, but the above definition contains the common terms and concepts used in most.

The media writer should be alert to stories that imply criminal or moral wrongdoing, that injure persons in their professions, or that hold them up to ridicule or scorn. Stories with such statements must be checked closely to make sure there are sound legal grounds for defense if challenged.

A red flag should go up when a story contains statements which attack a person's character, or imply that a person is insane, an alcoholic, a drug user or has a loathsome disease. Some words, such as swindler, whore, bandit, liar, crook and others which connote criminal or moral wrongdoing, can be dangerous.

The basic rule in all newsrooms should be to check out everything that is broadcast or printed. Negligence and careless mistakes can be costly.

In most instances the plaintiff in a libel suit must prove (1) that the person was identified directly or by inference, (2) that the offending material was printed or broadcast, (3) that the person's reputation was damaged and (4) that the publisher or broadcaster was at fault through actual malice, negligence or carelessness.

Three Major Defenses

Truth–Truth is generally considered the best defense in a libel suit. Therefore, the media writer should be certain that any potentially libelous statement can be proved true. The difficulty for the defendant might be in proving that the substance of a charge is true. A common problem arises when a newspaper or broadcast station believes it can avoid liability by attributing a libelous statement to a source.

In other words, if Jones calls Smith a crook–and the reporter puts that in a story–the reporter might have to prove that Smith is indeed a crook. Simply showing that Jones said it, would not constitute truth.

Some states specify that the defense of truth must also include justification or good motives for using the defamatory statements.

Privilege–The defense of privilege, broadly interpreted, covers fair and accurate reporting of public records and public proceedings such as those of courts, legislatures, city councils and other official bodies.

This defense is based on the concept that the public's business should be conducted in public. State laws vary on what are considered public records and public proceedings. The reporter should know the state law on privilege.

The mass media writer can report on these official proceedings even though defamatory remarks are made. The report must be fair and accurate, or the defense cannot be used.

Right of Fair Comment–This defense covers the right of persons to express opinions about public matters and persons in the public eye such as holders and seekers of public office, writers, entertainers, athletes and others who seek public attention. The opinions expressed must be based on facts and must be confined to matters of public interest or concern.

The opinions must extend only to an individual's work and not to his private life, and there must be no malice. For example, a book reviewer could say that a writer has little ability as a novelist and that his latest book is trash. This would probably be considered fair comment and not libelous. The reviewer probably could not write "Smith's book is trash because Smith was drunk while writing it."

Other Defenses

Some partial defenses should be mentioned. One is statute of limitations which varies from state to state, ranging from one to three years after the questionable material is printed or broadcast. Another is the defense of consent, where a person agrees to the publication or broadcast of libelous matter. The newspaper or broadcast station must have evidence of the consent.

A retraction can be published or broadcast which may serve to eliminate or reduce damages. In any event, a retraction can show lack of malice.

Malice

An important element to understand in libel cases is the concept of malice. Court rulings have defined malice as publishing or broadcasting material that is known to be false and defamatory, or of acting with flagrant disregard for the truth of the material.

The U.S. Supreme Court in 1964 in the so-called **New York Times** Rule said that public officials must prove actual malice to collect in libel suits. The concept of malice was later extended to public figures.

Both public officials and public figures must prove actual malice to win damages. Persons in these categories have a stronger, tougher hurdle than do private citizens. The courts have in recent years narrowed the definition of public figures, and the mass media writer should keep informed about rulings in this area. Often a libel decision can depend on whether the plaintiff is judged to be a private citizen or a public figure/public official. In all cases, however, it is important to be careful that provable malice is not present. If malice is present, the penalties for libel can be severe.

Invasion of Privacy

An area of growing concern for media writers is privacy. What constitutes invasion of privacy is far from clear. This area of law is slowly evolving as changes occur in state and federal statutes and court rulings.

Newsgatherers are generally protected from invasion of privacy suits when covering events and persons of public interest. Trespassing on private property, disclosing embarrassing private facts about a person without justification, or using a person's name or picture without consent for commercial purposes could be the basis for privacy suits. The mass media should not unnecessarily invade the privacy of persons.

Exercises: Chapter 12

I. Libelous statements made during testimony at a court trial may be published because of which major defense?

II. What are the three major defenses against libel?

III. What is libel?

IV. What is actual malice?

V. Explain the New York Times Rule.

Appendix A

Code of Ethics

(Society of Professional Journalists, Sigma Delta Chi, 1973)

The Society of Professional Journalists, Sigma Delta Chi, believes the duty of journalists is to serve the truth.

We believe the agencies of mass communication are carriers of public discussion and information, acting on their Constitutional mandate and freedom to learn and report the facts.

We believe in public enlightenment as the forerunner of justice, and in our Constitutional role to seek the truth as part of the public's right to know the truth.

We believe those responsibilities carry obligations that require journalists to perform with intelligence, objectivity, accuracy and fairness.

To these ends, we declare acceptance of the standards of practice here set forth:

RESPONSIBILITY: The public's right to know of events of public importance and interest is the overriding mission of the mass media. The purpose of distributing news and enlightened opinion is to serve the general welfare. Journalists who use their professional status as representatives of the public for selfish or other unworthy motives violate a high trust.

FREEDOM OF THE PRESS: Freedom of the press is to be guarded as an inalienable right of people in a free society. It carries with it the freedom and the responsibility to discuss, question, and challenge actions and utterances of our government and of our public and private institutions. Journalists uphold the right to speak unpopular opinions and the privilege to agree with the majority.

ETHICS: Journalists must be free of obligation to any interest other than the public's right to know the truth.

1. Gifts, favors, free travel, special treatment or privileges can

compromise the integrity of journalists and their employers. Nothing of value should be accepted.

2. Secondary employment, political involvement, holding public office, and service in community organizations should be avoided if it compromises the integrity of journalists and their employers. Journalists and their employers should conduct their personal lives in a manner which protects them from conflict of interest, real or apparent. Their responsibilities to the public are paramount. That is the nature of their profession.

3. So-called news communications from private sources should not be published or broadcast without substantiation of their claims to news value.

4. Journalists will seek news that serves the public interest, despite the obstacles. They will make constant efforts to assure that the public's business is conducted in public and that public records are open to public inspection.

5. Journalists acknowledge the newsman's ethic of protecting confidential sources of information.

ACCURACY AND OBJECTIVITY: Good faith with the public is the foundation of all worthy journalism.

1. Truth is our ultimate goal.

2. Objectivity in reporting the news is another goal, which serves as the mark of an experienced professional. It is a standard of performance toward which we strive. We honor those who achieve it.

3. There is no excuse for inaccuracies or lack of thoroughness.

4. Newspaper headlines should be fully warranted by the contents of the articles they accompany. Photographs and telecasts should give an accurate picture of an event and not highlight a minor incident out of context.

5. Sound practice makes clear distinction between news reports and expressions of opinion. News reports should be free of opinion or bias and represent all sides of an issue.

6. Partisanship in editorial comment which knowingly departs from the truth violates the spirit of American journalism.

7. Journalists recognize their responsibility for offering informed analysis, comment, and editorial opinion on public events and issues. They accept the obligation to present such material by individuals whose competence, experience, and judgment qualify them for it.

8. Special articles or presentations devoted to advocacy or the writer's own conclusions and interpretations should be labeled as such.

FAIR PLAY: Journalists at all times will show respect for the dignity, privacy, rights, and well-being of people encountered in the course of gathering and presenting the news.

1. The news media should not communicate unofficial charges affecting reputation or moral character without giving the accused a chance to reply.

2. The news media must guard against invading a person's right to privacy.

3. The media should not pander to morbid curiosity about details of vice and crime.

4. It is the duty of news media to make prompt and complete correction of their errors.

5. Journalists should be accountable to the public for their reports and the public should be encouraged to voice its grievances against the media. Open dialogue with our readers, viewers, and listeners should be fostered.

PLEDGE: Journalists should actively censure and try to prevent violations of these standards, and they should encourage their observance by all newspeople. Adherence to this code of ethics is intended to preserve the bond of mutual trust and respect between American journalists and the American people. (**Used by permission, Society of Professional Journalists, SDX**)

Appendix B

Copyreading Symbols

Copyreading symbols are used by reporters and editors who employ them in the form of pencil markings on typed news copy. They may be used to correct typographical errors, to make stylistic changes, or merely to add or delete words to improve the story.

Symbols	Explanation	Example
⌐	Use to indicate a paragraph	⌐Mayor Jones announced yesterday that his resignation will be effective July 1. ⌐He said he wanted to enter private law practice.
⌒	Bridging deleted copy between one line and another	Jones noted that during his tenure as mayor several zoning changes were ~~carefully planned, discussed and~~ passed by the Commission.

Symbols Explanations Examples

≡ or ⌐ Capital letters

≡jones said he would remain in the Dallas area. He expects to begin law practice in november.
                    ≡

/ lower case, or small letter

The former /Mayor said that he would miss his association with the local government.

⌐ Put in space

⌒ Reduce space

⌒ close up, taking out all spacing

He⌐praised city officials for their⌐dedicated work and said he hoped that they would look to him for help as n eeds a rose.

/ Delete single letter

═ Delete word or words

∨ Insert element

The mayor's famil/y will move to Richardson in the next week ~~month~~. He said they hoped to estab∨lsh their home by the beginning of school.

⌣ Insert word or words

The mayor⌃ the law firm of Nickels, Nickels and Nickels.
       (will join)

140

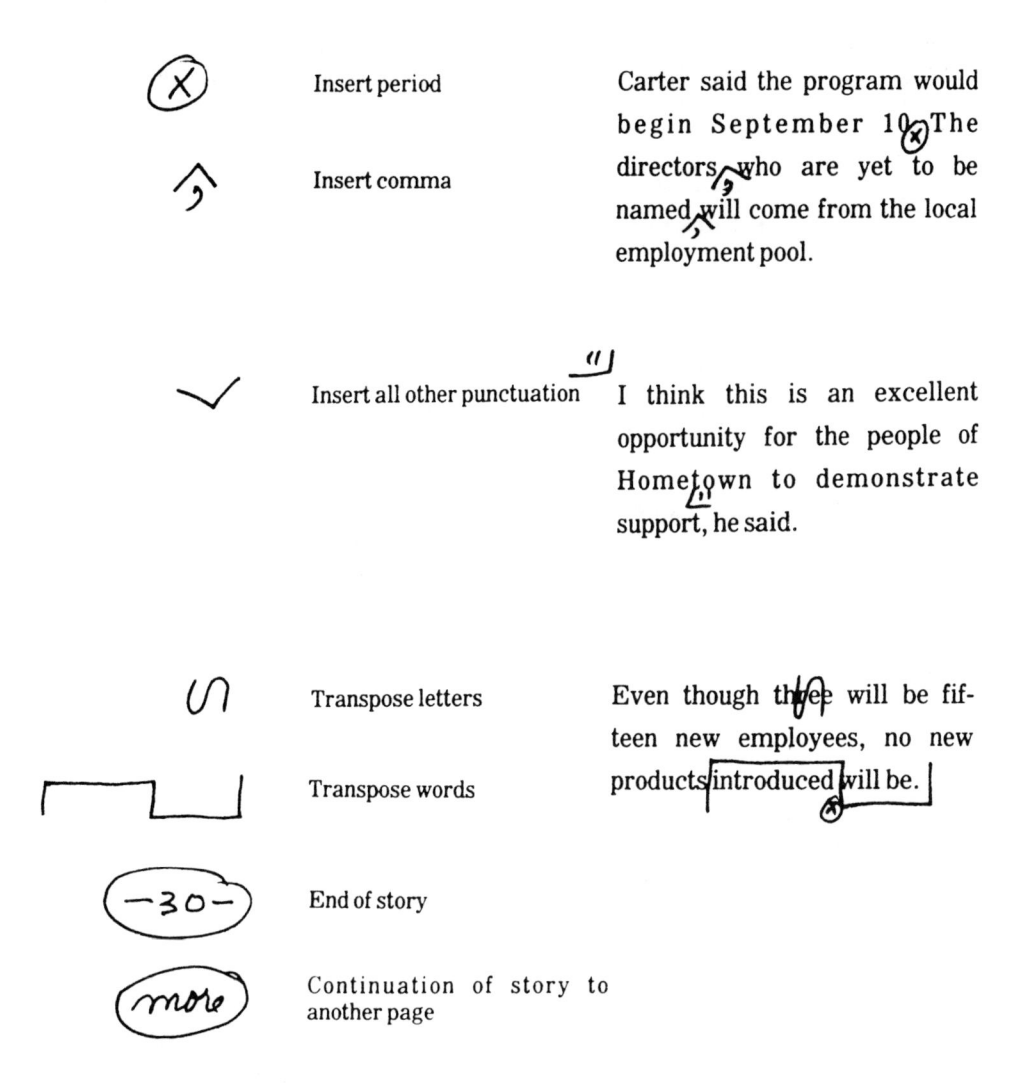

Symbols	Explanation	Example
Ⓧ	Insert period	Carter said the program would begin September 10Ⓧ The directors, who are yet to be named, will come from the local employment pool.
⌃,	Insert comma	
✓	Insert all other punctuation	I think this is an excellent opportunity for the people of Hometown to demonstrate support, he said.
∽	Transpose letters	Even though three will be fifteen new employees, no new products introduced will be.
⊔⊓	Transpose words	
-30-	End of story	
(more)	Continuation of story to another page	

Symbols	Explanation	Example
◯	Spell out numeral	Toda(8)students dropped...
◯	Put in numerals	Some(fifty)of them...
◯	Abbreviate	The workshop will be held (November)15.
◯	Spell out word	The governor will arrive in (Kan).(Fri.)

Appendix C

Copyreading for Broadcasting

Handwritten copyreading in broadcast copy should be limited to the four types of changes listed below. If a larger number of changes is needed, the copy should be retyped.

All broadcast copy should be turned over to the news director or newscaster only after it has been carefully copyread and corrected for accuracy, spelling, punctuation, grammar, style, taste, libel and slander.

Newscast copy must be "clean." If more than three changes are required, retype the copy. Handwritten copyreading symbols may distract the newscaster and cause reading difficulties.

Use the following guidelines in editing your copy:

1. To eliminate material from the copy:

The workshop is to start ~~promptly~~ at 10 Friday morning. ~~████████████~~. University students will be admitted free.

2. Misspelled Words: Correct by blocking out the word and writing it correctly. Do not block out individual letters or insert individual letters:

President ~~Reagan~~ *Reagan* warned the Soviet government that...

3. Minor changes may be made by blocking out material and inserting new copy:

The workshop ~~is to start~~ *begins* at 10 a.m. Friday morning...

4. It is permissible to insert limited new material in the copy:

The workshop is to ^*begin*^ at 10 a.m.

Appendix D

Spelling Demons

accidentally
accommodate
across
all right
apologize
assassin
athlete
athletic
baptize
battalion
believe
benefit
calendar
candidate
captain
cemetery
certain
changeable
committee
consensus
controversy
corner
coroner

criticize
decided
data
datum
definite
describe
desirable
develop
dietitian
dining
disappear
disappointed
divine
divide
dyeing
dying
embarrass
eighth
emphasize
equivalent
existence
familiar
February

fiery	opportunity
foreign	original
forty	paid (past of pay)
freshman (adj.)	parallel
government	particularly
grammar	perspiration
height	picnicked
hypocrisy	picnicker
immediately	planned
incidentally	possess
independent	precede
inoculate	privilege
interesting	procedure
its (pronoun)	proceed
it's (contraction)	professor
judgment	pseudonym
laboratory	questionnaire
laid (past of lay)	queue
led (past of lead)	rarefy
length	really
liaison	receive
libel	recognize
liquefy	remembrance
lose	replied
losing	respectfully
lovable	recommend
lying	respectively
marshal	restaurateur
meanness	salable
meant	seize
mischievous	sensible
mislead (present)	sergeant
misled (past)	sheriff
misspell	shining
morale	shriek
necessary	siege
neither	similar
occasion	similarity
occasionally	sizable
occurred	sophomore
omitted	straight

strength
stretch
summarize
superintendent
supersede
surprise
suspicious
theater
thorough
tied
truly
unnecessary
until
usage
using
usual
veteran
village
villain
Wednesday
weird
whether
wield
writing
abbreviate
abhorrence
abscond
absorption
absurd
accelerator
accessibility
accumulate
accustomed
achievement
acknowledgement
acoustics
acquaintance
adaptability
adjacent
admirable
admissible

advertise
advantageous
advice
advise
adviser
affidavit

alienate
align
allege
allocate
allotment
almanac
aluminum
amateur
ambiguous
analogous
analyze
animosity
annihilated
anoint
anonymous
Antarctic
antecedent
antidote
anxiety
appalling
apparatus
apparel
appellate
appetite
appreciate
appropriate
apropos
arguing
argument
arthritis
artificial
ascend
ascertain
aspirin

assault
assessment
atmosphere
attendance
audible
authentic
authoritative
auxiliary
bailiff
ballet
barbarous
beige
believable
belligerent
beneficial
benign
bigoted
bona fide
boulevard
bouquet
brilliant
broccoli
caffeine
caliber
camouflage
cancellation
cantaloupe
carburetor
catalog
caucus
cauliflower
chaperon, chaperone
chargeable
charismatic
chassis
chauvinistic
circumstantial
cite, site, sight
coincide
coliseum
collateral

colloquial
commemorate
commitment
committed
compatible
complimentary
complementary
conceive
conceivable
confer
conferred
conscious
conscientious (adj.)
consistency
conspicuous
contemptible
convalescent
convenience
copyright
corps
counterfeit
courteous
credibility
corroborate
crochet
curriculum
curricula
deceive
defendant
depositary (person)
depository (place)
descendant
desiccate
desperate
dilemma
diligent
dining-room (adj.)
diphtheria
discernible
disinfectant
dominant

drought
ecstasy
effect
affect
emanate
enunciate
envelop (verb)
envelope (noun)
environment
erroneous
exaggerate
excelled
excel
exercise
exhilarate
exorbitant
eyeing
fallacies
familiarity
financier
forehead
foresee
forward, backward, toward
fraudulent
fusillade
gauge
grandeur
gubernatorial
harass
hemorrhage
heresy
hoping
hopping (leaping)
humidity
hygiene
illiterate
immovable
impetuous
impromptu
inaugurate
indictment

indispensable
infinite
initiative
innocence
innocuous
innovate
insistence
interpretation
iridescent
irrelevant
irresistible
itinerary
impostor
legionnaire
maintenance
miniature
nickel
noticeable
occurrence
parliamentary
permissible
pimiento
poinsettia
practicable
prairie
pronunciation
rescind
resistance
rhythm
secede
significance
subtle
surveillance
synonymous
their (pronoun)
there (adverb)
they're (contraction)
tragedy
unanimous
vie, vied, vying

Appendix E
Sample News Story Format

(milnot feature
stubblefield
1-1-1-1-1)

    MILNOT, Okla./Mo.--Actually, there is no Milnot--Oklahome or Missouri. But there is a Milnot in each state.
    Confusing? You should have worked for the Milnot Co. several years ago when it really was confusing.
    Milnot produces canned milk products in a sprawling plant that precisely straddles the Oklahoma-Missouri state line at the west edge of Seneca, Mo. A quarter million pounds of raw milk come in each day from as far away as Eufaula, Okla.
    There are "state line" liquor stores, novelty stands, hamburger joints and even official state "welcome" signs. But rarely if ever are they truly ON the state line.
    Milnot is. Exactly.

(--more--)

milnot feature
stubblefield
2-2-2-2-2

A shiny brass stripe, about one inch wide is embedded in the brick floor of the plant to indicate the line. And a much larger brass plaque is mortared into the brickwork, paralleling the brass stripe, emblazoned with "OKLAHOMA" on the one side and "MISSOURI" on the other.

It was no fun and games thing. It had to be that way--at least some kind of accurate marker--when Milnot built its plant here in 1948.

The company, with its headquarters in Litchfield, Ill., didn't make a mistake in placing its building on the 10-acre tract. It was done deliberately so it could process and sell its products in both states.

"Federal regulations at that time prohibited interstate shipment of our product," manager Richard Day explained. "It remained that way until repeal in 1972 and now we ship to nearly 30 states."

Duplicate plant machinery to process and ship the product was installed on each side of the brass line, a marker carefully observed by management and workers. The only concession was for some heavy machinery that was placed on a steel track and moved from one side of the brass line to the other as it was needed.

There's still occasional kidding about the brass divid-

--more--

milnot feature
stubblefield
3-3-3-3-3

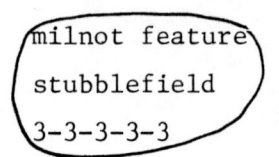

ing line, but all operations are carried on now without regard to the line.

Most of the work is done on the Oklahoma side of the brass line. Milk is received on the Oklahoma side, the laboratory is there, too, as are the butter making and evaporating process. Filling and sterilization is done on the Missouri side and labeling, boxing and warehousing are done on both sides.

The brass line is a symbol, not a barrier, now. Something to kid about, maybe a wager when OU is playing MU.

Day recalled that in the early days the two states disputed who was to get income taxes. One even wanted a breakdown on how much time was spent on each side of the line.

A woman employee set the tone of how it is today. "I tell my friends I work in Oklahoma and have to walk to Missouri to go to the restroom," she said. (Used by permission, The Tulsa World.)

--30--

Appendix F
PR Release

Southwest Cultural Heritage Festival
Oklahoma State University
Stillwater, OK 74078

Immediate Release

June 7, 1983

Chuck Fleming, Publicity
(405) 624-6354 Office
(405) 555-1234 Home

OSU GETS GRANTS FOR SOUTHWEST
CULTURAL HERITAGE FESTIVAL

STILLWATER, OKLA.----Oklahoma State University was recently awarded grants totaling $20,000 for support of the Southwest Cultural Heritage Festival scheduled Sept. 26-Oct. 6.

--more--

Festival Grants
2-2-2-2

The festival, in its third year at Oklahoma State University, attracts artists, musicians, scholars and writers from throughout the Southwest.

The Oklahoma Humanities Committee awarded a $10,000 grant to the festival, while the Oklahoma State University Foundation and the National Endowment for the Humanities provided $5,000 each.

Planning for the festival has been under way for nearly a year under the guidance of Michael J. Bugeja, festival director.

"We are pleased that the festival was funded again, Bugeja said, "because it will help us to continue this worthwhile project. We expect to bring to Stillwater some of the area's finest writers, artists, musicians, composers, historians, and scholars.

"Coordinators are in the process of working out travel plans with the visitors, and we can expect to have a final schedule by mid-July," Bugeja said.

The ten-day-long festival focuses on the culture of the Southwest, featuring art exhibits, films, musical and theater events, scholarly symposia, poetry readings, faculty and student presentations, and radio programs exploring the heritage of the area.

# # #

1-83

Index

Abstract words, 40
Acronymns and Initialisms, 84-85
Active voice
    verbs, 31, 126
Advertising,
    and 5 Ws and H, 109
    appeals, 109
    benefits of, 107
    criticisms of, 108
    defined, 107
    demographics, 109
    needs or desires, 109
    process of, 109-110
    psychographics, 109
Advertising copy
    descriptive, 110
    dialogue, 113-114
    emotional, 112-114
    factual, 110-112
    narrative, 112-113
    performance tests, 112
    predicament, 114
    promise, 111
    reason why, 110-111
    testimonial, 111
Attribution,
    in direct quotes, 45-46
    in indirect quotes, 46-47
    in continuous quotes, 46

Attribution,
    verbs of, 44-45
Biographical sources,
    Biography Almanac, 83
    Current Biography, 84
    Who's Who, 83-84
Black's Law Dictionary, 84
Books in Print, 87
Broadcast style,
    active verbs, 55-56
    attribution, 56-57
    conversational, 56
    numerals, 57
    present tense, 55
    punctuation, 57
    quotations, 57
    sentence structure, 56
    simplicity, 55
    sources, 56
Code of Ethics, SPJ, 135-137
Communication,
    defined, 1-2
    hurdles of, 4-6
    process of, 2-3
    theory of, 1
Computer-based data systems,
    Magazine Index, 87
    N.Y. Times Information
        Bank, 87

Concrete words, 40
Conflict,
    and human interest, 11
**Congressional Quarterly
    Weekly Report**, 80
Copyediting Symbols,
    Broadcast, 143-144
    Print, 139-142
Dictionaries,
    Webster's International, 84
    Webster's Collegiate, 84
Direct Observation,
    problems of, 65-66
Directed questions, 71
    disadvantages of, 71
Direct quotes,
    exactness of, 42
Directories,
    Ayer's Publications, 81
    **Broadcasting
    Yearbook**, 81
    Congressional Directory, 82
    **Editor & Publisher
    Yearbook**, 81
    Standard Rate & Data, 81
Editing,
    and language, 124-125
    and readability, 123-124
    sentence structure, 125
    as a process, 123-124
    procedures of, 128-129
    reference sources for, 124
Editorial Research Reports, 80
Fact finders,
    **Information Please
    Almanac**, 80
    World Almanac, 80
Facts on File, 79
Feature endings,
    climax, 100
    stinger, 101
    summary, 100
    un-ending, 101
Feature leads,
    descriptive, 95-96
    direct address, 97
    narrative, 94-95
    question, 96-97
    quotation, 96
    summary, 94
    teaser, 97-98
Feature story,
    brainstorming, 90
    color story, 91
    creativity, 90
    defined, 89
    development of, 91, 98-100
    entertaining, 91
    experiential, 90
    length of, 91
    subjective, 90
    theme development, 91
Feature types,
    experience, 92-93
    information, 93-94
    news, 91-92
    personality profiles, 93
    process, 92
First Amendment, 131
Frame of reference, 3
Hard news, defined, 92
Human interest,
    as a news value, 11
Humor and pathos,
    in human interest, 11
Impact,
    as a news value, 10-11
Information gathering,
    direct observation, 65-66
    the interview, 66-68
    secondary sources, 66

Interviews,
- and exact questions, 73-74
- and listening skills, 74-75
- and multiple questions, 74
- and notetaking, 77
- and objectivity, 72
- and questions with repetitive clauses, 74
- definitions of, 66
- for facts, 67
- pre-interview research, 68
- problems of, 75-76
- profile, 67
- story, 67
- talk-show, 67
- telephone, 76

Inverted pyramid,
- news story structure, 15-18
- purposes of, 15-17

Libel,
- defenses in, 132-133
- definition of, 131
- malice in, 133
- proof of, 132

Local directories,
- city directory, 85-86
- telephone directory, 86
- reverse directory, 86

Media, roles of, 1

Modifiers,
- problems with, 32-33

News, definition of, 9
News digests, 79-80
Newspaper Indexes,
- **NY Times**, 82

News story,
- chronological order, 18-19
- multi-dimensional, 24-26
- suspended interest form, 19

News values, combination of, 12
Non-directed questions,
- advantages, 70
- disadvantages, 70

Oddity, and human interest, 11
Parallel construction, 33
Passive voice, verbs, 32
Periodical indexes,
- **Education**, 83
- **PAIS**, 82-83
- **Readers' Guide**, 83

Pre-speech story, 48-49
Privacy, invasion of, 133
Public Relations,
- and theory, 117
- and media selection, 118
- and the media, 117
- and writing skills, 118-119
- news releases, 119
- news release example, 153-154

Prominence,
- as a news value, 10

Proximity,
- as a news value, 10

Quotation books, 85
- **Bartlett's**, 85
- **Oxford Book**, 85

Quotations,
- direct, 42-44
- indirect, 44
- partial, 43
- punctuation of, 43-44

Sample news story, 150-152
Selective exposure, 6
Selective perception, 6
Selective retention, 6
Sentence structure,
- news stories, 31-32

Soft news, defined, 92
Specificity and conciseness
- in writing, 40-41

Speech stories,
- lead emphasis, 47

multi-dimensional leads, 48
say-nothing lead, 47-48
Speeches,
coverage of, 47-48
Spelling demons, 145-149
Subject-verb-object
structure, 31
Subordination
in writing, 32
Summary leads,
who, 20
what, 20-21
when, 21
where, 21-22
why or how, 22-23
Timeliness,
as a news value, 9
Transition,
words used for, 23-24
Unity, in news story, 23
in news story, 23-24
Word books, 84
Roget's Thesarus, 84
Thesarus II, 84
Writing errors,
50 common, 33-40
Yearbooks,
Book of States, 87
Municipal Yearbook, 87
Statesman's Yearbook, 86